What's Being Said About...

Healing on the Horizon

Heather's words are a loving, living example of God's faithfulness — about how He is close to the broken and redeems pain. Grab a journal and pen and let your soul settle as she gently guides you towards hope and healing.

–**Laura Barringer**, Speaker and co-author of
A Church Called Tov and *Pivot*

In *Healing on the Horizon*, Heather masterfully guides readers through an empowering and compassionate 90-day devotional journey designed for those grappling with the scars of emotional abuse. This devotional transcends mere reflection; it becomes a trusted companion, allowing you to delve deep into the complexities of your experiences and emerge stronger and more resilient. Each day's entry is a blend of understanding and solace, providing practical insights and heartfelt prayers that nurture the healing process. With unparalleled empathy and wisdom, Heather illuminates a path towards reclaiming your sense of self and peace. This transformative guide is an essential resource for anyone seeking to heal and rediscover their strength, offering a hopeful horizon where healing, growth, and renewal await.

–**Brenda Stephens**, LPCC and author of *Healing from Narcissistic Mothers: A Daughter's Guide* and *The Narcissism Recovery Workbook*

This devotional is a resource that reminds us that we are not alone and that we have a safe haven in the arms of our Lord. For anyone who may be experiencing a toxic or abusive relationship and don't know where to run, these are the pages that will lead to your new beginning, your fresh start and your healing journey.

–**Ainsley Britain,** Author of *Don't Date a BooBoo Dude* and *The Enneagram for Teens*

In the aftermath of domestic abuse, it's hard to navigate life. In the midst of processing trauma and pain, Heather wrote the book she needed. Heather invites you to join her on a healing journey, offering daily devotions to help overcome the hardships and trauma of abuse.

–**Karen DeArmond Gardner,** Author of *Hope for Healing from Domestic Abuse*

Heather's *Healing on the Horizon* offers a way for someone who is in the midst of or has been through an abusive relationship to not only feel connected with another human being but to reflect on God's unwavering love written throughout Scripture. Heather's daily writings help name the abuser's tactics, acknowledge where you are or once were, encourage you to keep going, and remind you that you are not alone as you continue to heal; giving you the time and space to do so through personal reflection. There is a joy-filled life after abuse and trauma and Heather's words will guide you along the way as you begin, or continue on, your healing journey.

–**Stacey Szczepanski,** Author of *Unlocking Love: How Being Catfished Deepened My Faith and Led Me on a Journey to Wholeness*

Healing on the Horizon

Healing on the Horizon

A 90-Day Devotional Journey to Understand and Heal Your Heart, Mind, and Soul from Emotional Abuse

HEATHER N. JUSTICE

HOPE & JUSTICE
PUBLISHING

Healing on the Horizon
Copyright © 2024 by Heather N. Justice
All rights reserved.

All scripture references taken from the English Standard Version (ESV).

Published by Hope & Justice Publishing
ISBN: 979-8-99-13658-0-2
Cover design by Allison Raber
Author bio photo by Lauren Clarke
Edited by Megan Tatreau

This book is dedicated to my younger self.

When hope seemed distant and burdens felt too heavy to bear, this is what you needed and couldn't find. God had a greater plan unfolding and your unshakable faith allowed Him to reveal who He has always intended for you to be. You never once walked alone as you persevered through hardship and pain, and you deserve the love story you've prayed for. I'm proud of the woman you've become.

CONTENTS

Acknowledgements — 13

A Note from the Author — 15

Introduction — 19

Section One: Truth through Understanding — 21

Section Two: Truth through Prayer — 83

Section Three: Truth through Rediscovery — 145

Notes — 208

About the Author — 211

Acknowledgements

I couldn't have brought this book to life without the support of the many people who have walked alongside me throughout this journey.

First and foremost, thank you to my friends and family. Your unwavering encouragement has been a constant source of strength and motivation. Thank you for believing in me and in the purpose of this book. Every prayer, text message, and phone call were cherished! Thanks for joining me for the ride!

A special thanks to my book coach and developmental editor, Dori Harrell. Your insightful feedback and guidance were invaluable in shaping the manuscript.

Thank you to my copy editor, Megan Tatreau, for your meticulous attention to detail, ensuring the text was polished and precise.

A huge thank you to my incredible cover designer, Allison Raber, whose creativity brought my book to life with a cover that truly captures its essence. I will never forget crying happy tears when I saw what you created!

I extend my sincere appreciation to my talented friend and photographer, Lauren Clarke, for the stunning author photos. Thanks for posing me and getting all my best angles!

When I say it takes a village to write and publish a book, that's the truth! Thank you all for being an integral part of this journey.

A Note from the Author

Hello, sweet friend! I'm overjoyed you embraced the courage to pick up this book! After much therapy, prayer, healing, and rediscovery of my own, I wrote this book for you because this is the kind of resource I wished was available as I began breaking free from my emotionally abusive relationship in 2021. This type of devotional didn't exist, and I began to understand the dire need for it the more people I spoke with. I tried to find something to shed light on what I endured and how I could overcome it from a faith perspective. Fortunately, I found other methods of healthy healing and ways to rebuild myself and my life, but it has been a long journey. While I will focus on my romantic relationship in the following pages, it's crucial to recognize abuse can also manifest within friendships, family relationships, and work environments. Throughout this book, it is my desire to validate you, for you to know you were not alone then and you aren't alone now. You have purpose in this world, I'm glad you are here, and healing for your heart, mind, and soul is on the horizon. Before you dive in, here is an abbreviated version of my own story.

When I met my ex-boyfriend in October 2018 at a group meeting at work, our eyes locked, everyone else disappeared, the entire room went silent, and it was only him and me in this room full of people. At the conclusion of the meeting, I eventually introduced myself. He felt welcoming, warm, charming, and easy to converse with. He was incredibly good looking, previously in the Air Force, and older than me, all of which were attractive qualities in my eyes. We met for lunch at the end of October 2018 and afterwards, he asked for my number. Shortly after our first meetup, we went on several dates, and I'd never felt such intense emotion before. I can't tell you how many times I told my friends I thought I was in a real-life Hallmark movie.

We talked about our age difference (twelve years), marriage, and our future within a couple months of dating. Even though I didn't understand any of this at the time, he was mirroring me by making himself appear to be my soulmate, my perfect match. He was love bombing me by sending me sweet morning text messages, calling or FaceTiming me, meeting up with me at work, buying me flowers, and taking trips to quaint, romantic little towns. He was future faking me by talking about marriage, buying a house, living a life with me, him, and The Girls (aka my dogs–Zoey and Gia) in the not-so-distant future.

After three quick, short months, I was trauma bonded to him, even though I didn't know what a trauma bond was at the time. This type of bond happens rapidly with toxic people and is what continuously pulls someone back into an abusive situation. (You will learn about trauma bonding, love bombing, and future faking in the coming pages.) He broke up with me in December 2018, before visiting his family for Christmas. I was absolutely devastated. This was the first of many breakups and the start of the on-again-off-again roller coaster ride of my almost three-year abusive relationship. Yes, abusive. He emotionally and mentally abused me. It took what felt like an eternity for me to call it abuse, but now, I call it what it is.

When he returned from Christmas, we barely re-engaged in dating, only for our relationship to end again one month later. After this, I re-engaged four more times. It was a cycle of him cancelling trips or plans right before leaving, ignoring my calls and/or texts for hours on end—sometimes an entire day—giving me the silent treatment, not showing up when he said he would, or arriving hours late to any plans we made. This cycle was mixed with exceptionally good times because abusive relationships are not 100 percent bad 100 percent of the time. The good times involved things such as dancing in an alley to Christmas music, him encouraging me to start my homemade dog treat business, him bringing me flowers, and him being this seemingly patient, loving, vulnerable, trustworthy, safe place for me to land after an exhausting or frustrating day. These were the qualities I'd enthusiastically hoped and prayed for in my future spouse. And since I chose to be vulnerable and share this with him early on, this wasn't a surprise to him.

Throughout our relationship, I felt a "pulling" in my gut; something didn't feel quite right, but I couldn't put my finger on it. Then, as the last straw, I decided to run a background check and I found his expunged criminal record for Felony Battery, Domestic Battery by Strangulation. I was in disbelief. My relationship that started as a sweet little Hallmark movie took a sharp turn into a disturbing Lifetime movie, something I not once envisioned. He was never violent with me, never raised his voice at me, and never laid a hand on me in physical violence, but I didn't realize the amount and level of abuse, mentally and emotionally, I'd already suffered and the damage already done.

It was difficult to understand why God would allow me to go through such pain and heartache for such a lengthy period. My heart was extremely sick with hope deferred (Proverbs 13:12). I was hopeful once my abuser knew how much I loved him, he would be receptive of this love and revert to the man he was in the first three months of our relationship, and I'd be done with this broken carnival ride. But with this new information, it was a different story. He felt bizarrely unfamiliar to me, and I wasn't sure who he really was. I decided to confront him over FaceTime the next evening, and I told him I'd found his expunged record. He became quiet and said he wasn't going to talk about it over the phone with me and if I must talk about it anymore then we could talk about it in person. I told him there was no way I was going to talk to him in person knowing the information I found because I didn't know if he would do the same to me, and this was the first time he ever yelled at me. He said, "I CAN'T BELIEVE YOU. AFTER EVERYTHING WE'VE BEEN THROUGH. YOU THINK I WOULD DO SOMETHING LIKE THAT TO YOU? WOW. JUST WOW. GOODBYE!" and he hung up. After this, my stomach was in knots. It was the end. Emotions immediately overtook me. Shock, sadness, anger, desperation for closure and answers, defeat, confusion, and the list could go on. Thankfully, therapy was already scheduled for the same evening, and I filled my counselor in on the way everything transpired. She told me any time I was tempted to reach out to him, remember reading the word *strangulation* on my computer screen as a reminder not to contact him. Holding her advice close helped me remain focused on healing and moving forward.

God put the right people in my life at exactly the right time. His timing is perfect. He surrounded me with His love in the most evident ways. I prayed around the clock—while making my coffee, working, showering, walking my dogs Zoey and Gia—anywhere and everywhere. There were scriptures I held strong to throughout my healing, which you will see at the top of each section's introduction. I knew people were praying for me and those prayers were a huge part of my healing. The hugs from my mom and my friends, the time they sacrificed to be there for me, and the tears they shed right next to me were all part of my path to healing. After I learned more about abuse and what happened to me, I began to share my story of hope and tell how God restored me from brokenness and shame. I also began volunteering at a local domestic violence shelter to have the opportunity of loving and encouraging others who'd survived this insidious abuse.

God put this book on my heart, showing me there was purpose in my pain and my pain was not in vain. He gave me the words to help others, which I feel is a true calling and purpose from God. This quote by Oswald Chambers provides an honest summary of why I wrote this devotional: *"If through a broken heart God can bring His purposes to pass in the world, then thank Him for breaking your heart."* I give thanks to the Lord for the heartbreak, the growth through it, and the healing and understanding only He can provide.

I hope you finish this devotional with understanding and compassion for yourself and your experience and that you find things to bring forth joy and make you laugh so hard your sides hurt. But mostly, I hope you find a deeper and more meaningful relationship with Jesus than ever before. I hope you see Jesus doesn't blame you, and He will always love you, fill the void for you, and walk beside you through any and every situation, even if it feels insurmountable. I am excited for your future and for you to observe signs and wonders all around reminding you hope is forever found in Jesus. You are a child of the Most High!

I see you. I believe in you. You can do this.

Praying for hope, healing, and restoration,

Introduction

You are about to embark on a 90-day devotional journey of understanding, prayer, and rediscovery, which I pray results in hope, healing, and restoration for your heart, mind, and soul! I'll be the first to tell you from experience, it will be challenging. At times you will want to give up, call it quits, and resort back to what feels familiar and comfortable. Persevere! Keep going! I believe you will encounter beautiful moments far from what you unwillingly endured. I know this because I am living, breathing proof!

Healing on the Horizon is separated into three thirty-day sections:

Truth through Understanding – Section One aims to provide understanding about what happened during your abusive relationship. The intent is to provide insight into what the abuser's intentions were and what God's Word says about what happened. This section is represented by a hibiscus flower, which symbolizes wisdom and knowledge.

Truth through Prayer – Section Two serves as a guide for what to pray when words fall short. It is also to remind you of the open access you have to talk with God anytime, anywhere, in the same way you talk to your best friend. This section is represented by the lily of the valley flower, which signifies a Christian life.

Truth through Rediscovery – Section Three is packed full of activities to aid in the rediscovery of who you are by learning what you love to do and finding your joy in the mundane things of life once again. This section is represented by the lotus flower, which conveys rebirth, rediscovery, and overcoming adversity.

At the end of each day's devotion, there is a section titled,

**The Garden of Growth** – In this section, there is at least one prompt for you to reflect on and journal your answer. These questions are denoted by a dandelion, which is a symbol of survival, gentle strength, and resiliency.

While the book is written for you to work through one devotion per day to complete the devotional journey within ninety days, a handful of days you encounter may have more challenging content than others and require an additional day or two to complete. It's not a race, there is no timeline, and there is not a prize for finishing quickly or within exactly ninety days. Each person's journey of healing is different and unique.

Given there are prompts in The Garden of Growth section at the end of each day and within section three, many of the devotional exercises involve writing activities, I encourage you to use a separate journal specifically for these prompts and activities. This will ensure you reap the greatest benefit from your devotional journey by reflecting deeply and engaging fully. Journaling and documenting my experiences was helpful to my own healing. Journaling provided the opportunity to reflect on my growth, track how far I'd progressed, and be proud of the work I invested in myself. In Peter Lord's book *Hearing God*, he says, "When you see it, give expression to it–say something to someone about it, or write about it, or just say something out loud. You will then see more beauty than you have ever seen before."[1]

Finally, consider this book a gift to your emotional and mental health. I believe it will be worth it and give you strength to continue, especially when you finish, reflect on your journal entries, and recognize your growth. You are worth investing in. The time will pass whether you go on this journey or not, so why not do it? Brene Brown once said, "One day you will tell your story of how you overcame what you went through, and it will be someone else's survival guide." I hope you will include this book in your healing toolbox as a survival guide to get you through rough times, to understand what you've been through, and to know God never once left your side through it all.

Section One
Truth through Understanding

Jesus answered him, "What I am doing you do not understand now, but afterward you will understand."
John 13:7

Being in and leaving an emotionally abusive relationship was painfully confusing. I wasn't sure what happened to me the night it ended. It was extremely difficult to understand what I went through, how it affected me, and how I would ever find the strength to heal from something so incredibly complex; especially since I couldn't quite put my experience into words yet.

Section One provides you with thirty days of terms related to experiences that occur in many emotionally abusive relationships. Those terms are then refuted and denoted in bold font directly below the term with truths from the Word of God. Each day's devotion dives into a new term to provide a better understanding of the stages in the cycle of abuse (love bombing, devaluation, discard, hoovering). Additionally, each day explores the truth through scripture while propelling you forward in faith and reminding you of your resiliency and the promise of a more beautiful life than you could ever imagine.

DISCLAIMER:
Keep in mind as you read, many of the terms in Section One exist on a wide spectrum.

Day 1

Term: Abuser is Greater
God is Greater

He must increase, but I must decrease.
John 3:30

The abuser aims to gain control and make us feel less than, increasing themselves in power and taking away any control we have over our own lives, actions, and decisions. They want to be the sole authority figure in our lives. You may have noticed you feel less control over specific areas in your life and your abuser has displayed seemingly more power in those areas.

John the Baptist spoke John 3:30 during the overlap of his and Jesus' ministries. John understood who Jesus was, because God revealed it to him, and people were telling John that Jesus was baptizing people. John was quick to exclaim he himself was not the Christ, but Jesus was, and others *should* be getting baptized by Jesus and following His teachings. This was humble of John to say, as he realized the beauty and honor of having Jesus reign over his life as his Lord and Savior.

The similarities between the abuser and John or Jesus are nonexistent. Jesus has many names within the New Testament, and a name He is referred to as is *Lord*. Based on several definitions I reviewed, *lord* can be defined as someone who holds a position to command, direct, or dominate others; an authority figure, ruler or overseer. The abuser is not humble like Jesus and John but instead desires power and authority. The abuser views themselves as a lord or godlike person. We should not allow any human to be "god" over our lives. Jesus should be the sole reigning authority in our lives. If it feels like someone established power over you by taking the role of God themselves in your life, notice the feeling and don't disregard it. If someone established control over your life by cutting you down and diminishing you or your feelings and you have apprehension or an uneasy feeling in your gut, get curious, dig deeper about why the feeling is occurring, and trust the feeling.

When interacting with my abuser, the feeling of apprehension surfaced more times than I can count, and every time, I disregarded it. I thought it was my lack of experience in romantic relationships, but now I believe it was the Holy Spirit trying to communicate with me and protect me. Allow God to have full control over your life, so whenever these feelings arise, you can trust His guidance.

The Garden of Growth

Find today's Scripture in your favorite translation of the Bible (i.e. CSB, NIV, etc.). In your journal, write out the Scripture and reflect on what it means in your life and in your relationships.

Day 2

Term: Victim Mentality
God's Love

*"Therefore now, O LORD, please take my life from
me, for it is better for me to die than to live." And
the LORD said, "Do you do well to be angry?"*
Jonah 4:3–4

Living life with a victim mentality is a common mindset of abusers and there are multiple ways this presents. Some examples are (1) blaming others for their mistakes or feelings of misery, (2) constantly pointing out your personal flaws or problems within the relationship but not offering any solutions, (3) avoiding or being closed off to self-growth or self-reflection, (4) lacking self-awareness, and (5) wallowing in self-pity, acting as though they are suffering more than anyone else.

Jonah displayed a victim mentality and put the responsibility and blame on others for his happiness or lack thereof. The dialogue in Jonah 4:3-4 occurred between God and Jonah. Throughout the book of Jonah, Jonah was bitter, resentful, lacked accountability for his sins, didn't want to change or think there was anything to change, was jealous of Ninevah's blessings, was unforgiving, and made his suffering sound worse than what anyone else was enduring.

The abuser is like Jonah—bitter, resentful, jealous of others' accomplishments or favor, unforgiving, and holding tightly to the victim mentality. Being with someone identifying with this mentality is dangerous, especially when you are kind, caring, and self-reflective, because they will take advantage of your empathy, kindness, and generous spirit.

With my abuser, I continuously tried to make our relationship work because, sometimes, I felt sorry for *him*. He was well-versed at gaining sympathy—he certainly appeared to suffer more than everyone else and fall prey to the world constantly plotting against him. I believed if I could simply show him how much God loved him and how much I loved him, then his mindset would change. I didn't understand he didn't desire change.

Rest assured no matter how much you tried to show them love and how hard you tried to make it work, it wouldn't change them or the long-term outcome. It wouldn't change because, regardless of your hardworking efforts, the abuser built a reality *they* live in. They believe when anything happens to them, it is the fault of someone else and it doesn't have anything to do with their words or actions. They lack accountability. For the sake of clarity, there is a difference between adopting a victim mentality and being an innocent victim of circumstances. It's crucial to understand you were affected by someone else's harmful actions, which made you a victim. However, it's important to not allow the evil you endured to dominate and control your life and become trapped in a victim mentality.[2] Stay strong, consistent, and know healing is coming!

The Garden of Growth

Find today's Scripture in your favorite translation of the Bible (i.e. CSB, NIV, etc.). In your journal, write out the Scripture and reflect on what it means in your life and in your relationships.

Day 3

Term: Shame
No Condemnation

There is therefore now no condemnation for those who are in Christ Jesus.
Romans 8:1

Shame is among the earliest emotions referenced in the Bible (Genesis 2:24-3:10, 21). Feeling shame is familiar to abusers. In fact, shame is often at the root of who they are, but most will not admit to it, as it requires vulnerability and facing fears and guilt head on. Even though many abusers come off as egotistical, they struggle deeply with having a strong sense of self and healthy levels of self-esteem. Instead of addressing the root cause of why they are feeling shame and how it affects their relationships with romantic partners, friends, family, or colleagues, they blame, criticize, and cut down others around them in order to make themselves feel better. This allows the abuser to view others on the same level as themselves and see others as just as flawed as they are. The *Therapy and Theology* podcast describes shame in this way: **Self-Hatred At My Expense.**[3]

Romans 8:1 gives believers comfort. It explains if we repent and are vulnerable, Christ will forgive us and wash away any shame, and we will have a better future for it. Shame is self-condemnation, and scripture explains there is *no* condemnation when we are walking with Jesus. For the abuser, because their life is rooted in shame, their lack of willingness to take accountability and to be vulnerable is unfamiliar territory.

Did you ever notice your abuser become defensive after you provided constructive criticism when they shared a difficult situation they were part of? What about after you shared an accomplishment with them? Did they make a comment close to, "You did well, but what you could have done even better is..." Or maybe, unconvincingly, they said your accomplishment was cool, but they brought the conversation back to themselves and an accomplishment of their own rather than celebrating you. These are all shame-based reactions having everything to do with the abuser and nothing to do with the amazing, intelligent, and talented person you are.

My abuser would often be frustrated by situations at work, but he would rarely talk about them. On the occasion he did, I would listen but also tried to offer advice on how he could help himself and improve the situation. Following our conversation, I would often get "punished" with the silent treatment, leaving me to wonder if he was mad at me or if he was going to break it off with me because he felt as though I didn't take his side in support of him. I was constantly waiting for the next shoe to drop.

Friend, I've got to tell you—when your abuser is full of shame, it's not your responsibility to fix them. In fact, *you* can't fix them. Only God can fix them, and it's up to the abuser to be vulnerable, take accountability for their actions, face their guilt and shame head on, and walk in a no-condemnation bond with Jesus Christ. Release yourself from the burden of fixing them. It's time to focus on deepening your connection with Jesus and yourself. You've got this!

The Garden of Growth

Find today's Scripture in your favorite translation of the Bible (i.e. CSB, NIV, etc.). In your journal, write out the Scripture and reflect on what it means in your life and in your relationships.

Day 4

Term: Projection
Self-Reflection

*"Why do you look at the speck of sawdust in your
brother's eye and pay no attention to the plank in your
own eye? How can you say to your brother, 'Let me take
the speck out of your eye,' when all the time there is a
plank in your own eye? You hypocrite, first take the plank
out of your own eye, and then you will see clearly to
remove the speck from your brother's eye."*
Matthew 7:3-5

Projection, as defined in the psychology world, is "the process of displacing one's feelings onto a different person, animal, or object."[4] This is a defense mechanism the abuser uses—they often project their own insecurities or actions onto others. As you read yesterday, the abuser doesn't have a strong sense of self, but they will not own it, which is where projection comes in. They project onto others to avoid exposing their own insecurities.

An example of projection presenting often with abusers in romantic relationships is when the abuser accuses their partner of cheating when *they* are the person being unfaithful. I didn't have this experience of projection, but I did learn after the final breakup he was in fact cheating on me with several different women throughout our time together.

Matthew 7:3-5 is from Jesus' Sermon on the Mount. He went to the top of the mountain and His disciples came to hear Him teach. In these verses, Jesus was teaching about judging others and how we should correct our own faults before pointing out the faults of others. This sermon would not be received well by the abuser as they are overly critical of others. The abuser lacks the ability to look inward and self-reflect, which is the root cause of why they often project onto others.

Evaluate the relationship. If this sounds familiar, keep in mind projection is part of the abuser's mentality and personality. You can self-reflect and look inward as Jesus instructed the disciples to do in His Sermon on the Mount. Self-reflection and looking inward helps you to heal from the abuse you encountered for several reasons: you can (1) take notice of what you're feeling and identify when you need support from friends or family, (2) reclaim your power by acknowledging your resiliency and strengths, (3) process your emotions, and (4) more easily identify triggers and negative thought patterns. Each step you take brings you closer to restoration and peace. Continue to nurture your well-being. All these things are part of healing. Keep growing, my sweet friend.

The Garden of Growth
• •

 Find today's Scripture in your favorite translation of the Bible (i.e. CSB, NIV, etc.). In your journal, write out the Scripture and reflect on what it means in your life and in your relationships.

Day 5

Term: Pathological Lying
God's Delight

Lying lips are an abomination to the Lord, but those who act faithfully are his delight.
Proverbs 12:22

Pathological lying is common in emotionally abusive relationships. Abusers use lies to manipulate and create the reality they want to live in. If we are honest, we all lie from time to time; however, lying exists on a spectrum. Someone who lies pathologically creates detailed, complicated, and dramatic lies with little to no regard for who they hurt along the way. Someone who is not a pathological liar might tell a white lie to their friend about liking their haircut or outfit in order to spare their friend's feelings.

Do you recall any time(s) with your abuser when you'd ask a question and would get an excessively long, drawn out answer, with too many details for you to recall later? This situation is typical when dealing with a pathological liar. The lies may also have been paired with an Oscar-worthy performance for dramatics.

When this type of behavior arises, it can feel as though we are the problem, or we begin questioning why we have trouble trusting what our abuser is saying. Don't disregard these feelings—get curious to the point of asking clarifying questions. I believe this is the Holy Spirit working in our lives, prompting us and giving us a sign to pay attention to things going on around us.

Proverbs 12:22 says lying lips are an abomination to the Lord. Synonyms of *abomination* include *disgust, disgrace, repulsion,* and *horror*. The Lord wants His people to act faithfully and truthfully! The abuser can sometimes be referred to as a wolf in sheep's clothing (Matthew 7:15), meaning they are ravenous monsters on the inside but appear kind, honest, vulnerable, and caring on the outside. It can be difficult to identify these types of people as they appear a certain way to most people and a different, abusive, and toxic way to those closest to them. Most live a life built on lies and secrets, sometimes even a double life.

It is vital to acknowledge the goodness of God. He is a good, good Father who is constantly watching out for us and what's best for our lives. If it felt like you were dealing with someone exuding these characteristics of lies and secrets, ask God to reveal the truth to you and be willing to open your eyes, ears, and mind to what God wants to reveal for you to have the best for your life.

The Garden of Growth

Find today's Scripture in your favorite translation of the Bible (i.e. CSB, NIV, etc.). In your journal, write out the Scripture and reflect on what it means in your life and in your relationships.

Day 6

Term: Lacking Empathy
God Cares

Jesus wept.
John 11:35

Empathy plays a huge role in connecting with others. This is not an emotion an abuser has the ability to express. Having minimal or low empathy leads to friction with others and is a reason for their lack of meaningful, deep, and vulnerable connection. The abuser doesn't consider how their behavior affects people and often doesn't care if it negatively impacts others.

I recall when I planned a movie-themed Saturday date night. It was on the calendar for weeks, but my abuser called me the night before and told me his sister and her kids wanted to visit over the same weekend and he told them to go ahead and come down. I explained to him how much this disappointed me since he knew the amount of time and effort I'd put into our weekend plans, but he couldn't understand why. I tried to explain to him by giving him a scenario he would understand to no avail. He said we could just reschedule our plans. Then, he proceeded to say, "Well, we *are* going to have to eat while they are here. I guess you could join us for lunch tomorrow if you want." This invitation didn't seem welcoming; rather, it felt obligatory. If this lack of empathy is something you have felt, I'm sorry. I know first-hand how it felt, and it was a minimizing feeling. I felt insignificant, second choice, a burden, or like I was constantly in the way.

John 11:35 is made up of two words encompassing significant meaning: Jesus wept. Simple, right? This Scripture comes during the time Lazarus was sick and his sisters, Mary and Martha, sent a message to Jesus asking Him to come heal their brother. Once Jesus arrived, Lazarus was already deceased for four days. The crowd explained to Jesus they'd already put Lazarus in the tomb, but they could take Him to where he was buried. Jesus followed along to the tomb, and then He wept. Jesus wept for two reasons: (1) He was grieving for the fallen world, for sorrow and death, and (2) He felt the pain of the people around Him. He felt empathy for those who were experiencing the loss of a friend and brother. Jesus loves us, He understands our pain better than anyone else ever could, and He grieves right alongside us. You can stand strong knowing Jesus dealt with the maximum amount of disappointment and understands empathy at the core.

The Garden of Growth

 Find today's Scripture in your favorite translation of the Bible (i.e. CSB, NIV, etc.). In your journal, write out the Scripture and reflect on what it means in your life and in your relationships.

Day 7

Term: Giving with a Goal
God's Free Gift

For by grace you have been saved through faith. And this is not your own doing; it is the gift of God, not a result of works, so that no one may boast.
Ephesians 2:8-9

Everyone feels loved in different ways. As discussed in Gary Chapman's book, *The Five Love Languages*,[5] it's not unusual for people to have different love languages (words of affirmation, physical touch, gifts, acts of service, or quality time). An abuser can use gift giving as a way of manipulation, a way to get something they want, or to take the focus off an unacceptable behavior.

My abuser would often use giving as a form of manipulation. As our time together progressed, I saw him less and less each week. By the time the following instance occurred, he was committed to seeing me one day a week, which was typically Saturdays or Sundays, not a weekday. He asked during a particular week on a weekday if he could stop by. He showed up with flowers and a card in hand. I immediately put the flowers in a vase, read the card, and thanked him for the wonderful, meaningful surprise, expressing excitement that I would get to see him more than once in the same week. Then, he dropped the bomb on me: he was going to visit his brother and we wouldn't see each other over the weekend. I then understood his intention in giving me the flowers and the card was to try to alleviate the negative emotions brought forth by the news. It wasn't easy for me to digest, especially since my love languages are quality time and physical touch, and I was already spending a minimal amount of time with him.

The pain of feeling I wasn't important to him and knowing he was choosing to give me the bare minimum was a hard pill to swallow. What was more heartbreaking was to learn the sweet gestures or gifts he gave came with strings attached, which is unlike the free gift of salvation from our heavenly Father.

Ephesians 2:8-9 clearly explains God gives the free, no-strings-attached gift of salvation. He doesn't require us to perform a certain number of good deeds in exchange for it. It is a free gift God grants to us by grace through faith. To me, it is incredibly freeing knowing God doesn't expect me to perform certain tasks on a list or a specific number of good works to be accepted into His kingdom as His beloved child. The same cannot be said when enmeshed in a relationship with an abusive person.

There is a life exceptionally better for you! Please know God loves you and there are no strings attached to the love and comfort He provides.

The Garden of Growth

Find today's Scripture in your favorite translation of the Bible (i.e. CSB, NIV, etc.). In your journal, write out the Scripture and reflect on what it means in your life and in your relationships.

Day 8

Term: Mirroring
Fully Known

*O Lord, you have searched me and known me!
You know when I sit down and when I rise up;
you discern my thoughts from afar.*
Psalm 139:1-2

When you look into a mirror, your image is reflected back to you. Mirroring is a tactic abusers use as a way of manipulation to make others feel more connected to them. It provides a sense of safety and familiarity to the other person when the abuser replicates the same gestures, body language, and speaking patterns and even shares the same hobbies and interests.

Early on, I recall feeling my abuser embodied me in male form. We ironically shared many little things in common, but it didn't cross my mind he could be mirroring me to make himself appear as if he were my perfect match. Once I learned about mirroring and understood it was a form of manipulation, I realized mirroring was his way of building a bond with me, encouraging me to open up and share my vulnerabilities and insecurities with him. This allowed him to gather information about me, which he later used against me. Now I know, when I started feeling an unimaginable bond with the abuser (the two of us were strangely alike and shared many similarities), it felt as though I was entering into a relationship with someone who knew the deepest parts of me—fully knew me and still deeply loved me. This feeling aligns with what was mentioned in day one's devotion regarding the abuser embracing a godlike, all-knowing persona.

It is alarming to think someone can adapt their actions with utter ease to fit a situation with manipulation as the motivating factor. Psalm 139:1-2 was spoken by David as he understood nothing, not even what was inside, could be hidden from God. While my abuser paid close attention to things about me to learn how to mirror me, God knows the deepest parts of us, loves us, and doesn't use manipulation as a way of gathering information to use against us later. I love and appreciate God knowing absolutely everything about us and not using the knowledge to exploit us but instead to refine us, love us deeper, and fill any empty voids inside of us! His omniscience brings comfort, knowing He sees and understands every facet of our being and His intentions are pure. Allow God's love to mend what is broken and His grace to lead you into a future filled with hope and wholeness.

The Garden of Growth

Find today's Scripture in your favorite translation of the Bible (i.e. CSB, NIV, etc.). In your journal, write out the Scripture and reflect on what it means in your life and in your relationships.

Day 9

Term: Love Bombing
Loving Truthfully

*Faithful are the wounds of a friend;
profuse are the kisses of an enemy.*
Proverbs 27:6

Love bombing is the first stage of the abuse cycle and is a grooming technique abusers use to receive admiration and be viewed as the perfect person. It also makes it easier for the abuser to obtain people's idolization. Love bombing can happen at various stages of a relationship but often occurs quickly after initially meeting. Love bombing can be exhibited as intense displays of affection, grandiose gestures, and over-the-top admiration. It can feel flattering in the beginning, especially if it's a foreign experience.

Hands down, my abuser knew the right words to say to make him appear to be the man I'd prayed for years would come along. In the beginning when we were out together, he would treat me with such unrealistic perfect kindness. I later found out some of my family and friends would cringe when they saw it, realizing how insincere it was. However, I thought he was the most wonderful knight in shining armor. I could only have dreamed of being treated with such love and compassion, but over the next several months, it all faded, and I yearned to see the man I first met.

If you were love bombed and missed the signs the way I did, you probably also engaged with friends who begged for you to open your eyes to what was happening. When there are deep emotional wounds involved and/or a longing to feel deep, genuine love, especially if this wasn't the norm for your childhood, it is hard to differentiate between what's real or fake.

Proverbs 27:6 explains love is more than always being a "yes man" and saying what the person wants you to say. Love is more than constant flattery and praise, grandiose gestures, and gifts. This Scripture is teaching the biblical principle that when real love exists, a person who loves you will be willing to have hard conversations because they have your best interest at heart. They will be kind, but they won't *only* flood you with praise or *only* give you gifts via grandiose gestures, as it's not sustainable and it's disingenuous.

I assure you, why or how you entered this entanglement has nothing to do with your level of intelligence. You didn't know what was coming or how it would affect you. You desired the truest, purest form of love, and you can't blame yourself for wanting a beautiful love story! Your resilience and courage to seek healing are admirable. Embrace your journey with compassion for yourself, knowing that brighter days are ahead.

The Garden of Growth
· ·

Find today's Scripture in your favorite translation of the Bible (i.e. CSB, NIV, etc.). In your journal, write out the Scripture and reflect on what it means in your life and in your relationships.

Day 10

Term: Idealization
One True God

He feeds on ashes; a deluded heart has led him astray, and he cannot deliver himself or say, "Is there not a lie in my right hand?"
Isaiah 44:20

Idealization often goes hand in hand with love bombing. In the beginning of a relationship, the abuser puts you on a pedestal, and you become their idol. They want to learn all they can about you, then take the information and contort it into this perfect version of you in their minds. From there, they are only interacting with their idealized version of you, not with you as an external human being.

My first official date with my abuser was a weekend meet up at a local coffee shop. We were there for four hours talking. He asked me an exorbitant number of questions about myself and my life, my interests, hobbies, family, etc. I found it nice how inquisitive he was about me, and I thought he was genuinely trying to get to know me. After our breakup and learning what I underwent, I thought back on many conversations with him and realized I was usually answering his questions. Before I could even finish the answer to one, he was already asking me another. If I did ask him questions, his answers were brief, and he would revert to asking me questions.

Isaiah 44:20 explains those who lived in delusion worshipped idols, which filled them with false hopes of being delivered, much like eating ashes, which provide no substance or nourishment. The Scripture goes on to explain, people who chose to idolize are deceived and cannot be delivered by their own power and must seek out saving and deliverance from God. In addition, 1 Corinthians 8:4 states idols don't exist and there is only one true God. With this understanding, it became obvious what my abuser was doing by idealizing me was unhealthy and wouldn't have led to a fulfilling future together.

Detecting this behavior with someone new can be difficult. I believe it is innate for us to want to believe the best in people or trust them until they give us a reason not to; however, it's a slippery slope with abusive people. I genuinely wish I could be sharing a cup of coffee with you, validating you, and giving you the opportunity to take your turn asking questions. I pray you take the chance to put yourself out there and give it another try, if you want to. If you do, you will be more equipped with information you didn't have before and long-lasting, true encouragement from God's Word. Keep turning these pages!

The Garden of Growth

Find today's Scripture in your favorite translation of the Bible (i.e. CSB, NIV, etc.). In your journal, write out the Scripture and reflect on what it means in your life and in your relationships.

Day 11

Term: Breadcrumbing
Eternal Hope

"Let what you say be simply 'Yes' or 'No'; anything more than this comes from evil."
Matthew 5:37

When I think of breadcrumbing, I think of the story *Hansel and Gretel* when Hansel laid breadcrumbs on the trail in the forest so he and his sister could find their way back home. However, the term breadcrumbing in the way of abuse comes from the abuser using small beacons of hope, such as a sweet text message, random dates, or the occasional phone call because you were on their mind, to keep people holding onto hope of their changed behavior. The breadcrumbs are usually just sufficient enough to keep someone from leaving all together.

My abuser carried out significant breadcrumbing. I shared my feelings with him often, as you would in a healthy relationship, which made him aware of when I was at my breaking point of wanting to walk away. When this happened, he would follow up with an impromptu date or a long text message about how thankful he was for me and how he would work on things. He would cast his line out, giving me some kind of hope to hang on to and convincing me to believe things would improve. But of course, they didn't improve long-term.

Matthew 5:37 makes it clear we should not create an environment of confusion or instability. We should mean what we say and say what we mean—be a person of our word. Doing anything else is not kind and is a byproduct of evil. Abusers are hot and cold, on and off, and yes and no. There is confusion and instability with these types of people. It leads to frustration, exhaustion, rejection, and anxiety for the person on the receiving end of their behavior. I know this from personal experience.

The breadcrumbs provided me with hope the man from the beginning of my relationship would return. An abuser uses many of the terms you've read about up to this point as tactics to deceive and keep people hanging on even though the abuser knows they don't intend to make a lasting change. Don't be ashamed if breadcrumbing is what kept you unhealthily attached for longer than you wanted. But now, you're free, and if you're not free yet, I believe you will be soon! You're learning what happened, and by the grace of God, there is going to be a beautiful life for you with this knowledge.

The Garden of Growth
. . . .

Find today's Scripture in your favorite translation of the Bible (i.e. CSB, NIV, etc.). In your journal, write out the Scripture and reflect on what it means in your life and in your relationships.

Day 12

Term: Future Faking
God's Plan

*"For I know the plans I have for you," declares the Lord,
"plans for welfare and not for evil, to give you a future
and a hope."*
Jeremiah 29:11

Future faking occurs when the abuser makes promises about the future to gain immediate benefits. For example, they might say you'll meet their family soon but never arrange it, promise to call you back but don't follow through, or talk about vacationing together without taking any steps to make it happen.

This was a tactic my abuser used regularly. I first noticed future faking a few weeks into our relationship. Remember a few devotions back I mentioned he reminded me of the male version of myself and we shared oodles of little things in common? About three weeks in, before leaving my house after a date, he said, "We're on the fast track, babe." This was after we discussed how we envisioned our future. We were both older (he was twelve years older than me) and he was mindful I was in a place where I didn't want to waste any time dating "the wrong person." He made comments about our future together and painted a picture of how our life would look after we were married. Of course, I later learned he didn't have any intention of marrying me (thank God for blessings in disguise, but I didn't realize the blessing at the time).

Through the years, I've treasured Jeremiah 29:11, as God promises He already knows what our future holds. Despite what we are going through right now, it is a future of hope! This Scripture is from the letter the prophet Jeremiah wrote to the exiles of Babylon, reminding them and providing great assurance of God's intentions to shed future blessings in the land of Israel. The abuser makes false promises and doesn't keep their word. They utilize this form of manipulation to maintain your attachment to empty commitments regarding their future involvement in your life.

This was a tough lesson to learn. I realized my abuser wasn't consistent in what he said, and he didn't follow through regularly with what he told others. Consistency is a key determinate to verify if you experienced future faking. It's important to trust your instincts, and if you sense someone is making promises and consistently not following through, it's perfectly valid to ask questions. Take time between being together—don't give them vulnerable access immediately. Talk to God, gain clarity if you're feeling uncertain, and know God has a plan for you to have a prosperous future containing good and not evil.

The Garden of Growth

 Find today's Scripture in your favorite translation of the Bible (i.e. CSB, NIV, etc.). In your journal, write out the Scripture and reflect on what it means in your life and in your relationships.

Day 13

Term: Triangulation
The Good Portion

Now as they went on their way, Jesus entered a village. And a woman named Martha welcomed him into her house. And she had a sister called Mary, who sat at the Lord's feet and listened to his teaching. But Martha was distracted with much serving. And she went up to him and said, "Lord, do you not care that my sister has left me to serve alone? Tell her then to help me." But the Lord answered her, "Martha, Martha, you are anxious and troubled about many things, but one thing is necessary. Mary has chosen the good portion, which will not be taken away from her."
Luke 10:38-42

Triangulation is a form of manipulation an abuser uses to protect their ego and is when a third person is brought into the picture as a way for the abuser to remain in control.[6] Envision a triangle. The bottom points are the triangulated individuals, and the top point is the abuser. There is typically not any communication between the two triangulated individuals, except through the abuser.[6] The abuser uses triangulation to avoid accountability, obtain power, or to gain admiration.[7]

My abuser used a woman in his office to triangulate. I constantly competed for his attention. I knew this woman before he was employed there and communicated with her from time to time. I knew her to be an attractive, kind, and bubbly person. I frequently asked if he wanted to meet for lunch or take a walk together during a break and he would tell me he was going for a walk with his female colleague to vent about his work frustrations. He knew it made me uncomfortable because I'd previously expressed my feelings to him, but he continued doing it, and I eventually accepted it.

In Luke 10:38-42, Martha attempted to triangulate when she welcomed Jesus into her home and was focused on being the most remarkable hostess, whereas Mary was focused on Jesus and His teachings. Martha was slaving away, and she didn't feel she was being admired the way she'd anticipated. Martha's ego was probably bruised as she wasn't being viewed as "the favorite." Instead of addressing her sister directly, she approached Jesus, highlighting the effort she was pouring into His visit compared to her sister's apparent lack of effort. It's as if she hoped Jesus would respond affirmatively, perhaps saying, "Yes, Martha, I understand. Thank you for your efforts. Mary, please go help your sister immediately." However, Jesus responded by telling Martha that Mary was doing what was right by listening to His teachings rather than looking for adoration and praise.

Triangulation brings about jealousy, drama, unhealthy communication patterns, and creates conflicts. Ultimately, the abuser gets their needs met by receiving attention (whether good or bad), creating drama, and holding the key to control the direction of the drama. It's unfortunate the abuser uses these tactics to get their needs met, leaving others to suffer at the hand of their abuse. I know this insidious abuse tore you down bit by bit, but the rebuild is coming. God hasn't given up on you, so don't give up on yourself!

The Garden of Growth

 Find today's Scripture in your favorite translation of the Bible (i.e. CSB, NIV, etc.). In your journal, write out the Scripture and reflect on what it means in your life and in your relationships.

Day 14

Term: Isolation
Gather Together

And let us consider how to stir up one another to love and good works, not neglecting to meet together, as is the habit of some, but encouraging one another, and all the more as you see the Day drawing near.
Hebrews 10:24-25

Abusers often seek to isolate individuals from friends and family, making the abuser the only person in their life. This gives the abuser more control as those same friends and family become distant memories.

My abuser didn't outright isolate me as I understand others have suffered, but he would make plans with me for the weekend and when the day arrived, he would delay the time later and later in the day and eventually say it was too late to do anything. This resulted in it being too late for me to make plans with anyone else, making it a wasted day. I stayed at home and chose not to spend the day with my friends or my family since I'd blocked out time to spend with him. Also, because of the complete exhaustion I felt from being a passenger on the emotional roller coaster, when I wasn't spending time with him, I chose to rest or be alone.

Hebrews 10:24-25 reminds us not to live in isolation and to congregate with others often. This Scripture explains gathering together pushes us to love, help, and encourage others. Abusers want people to remain as isolated as possible because it is easier to keep the abuse a secret. It also keeps the person suffering the abuse in the dark about what is ultimately happening to them, as it's not easy to recognize the abuse when you're constantly in the midst of it.

It's no wonder God doesn't want us to be isolated. When we are isolated it's unequivocally easier for Satan to prey upon our weaknesses, fill our minds with lies, and lead us further down the wrong path. Additionally, when we aren't in community with likeminded people, allowing them to speak truth and life to us, we will stay connected to the abuser longer. In the same way iron sharpens iron, good friends can sharpen one another both intellectually and theologically (Proverbs 27:17). Gather often with those who love and care about you and have your best interests in mind. God loves when we gather with others and glorify Him together.

The Garden of Growth

Find today's Scripture in your favorite translation of the Bible (i.e. CSB, NIV, etc.). In your journal, write out the Scripture and reflect on what it means in your life and in your relationships.

Day 15

Term: Devaluation
Love One Another

This is my commandment: Love each other in the same way I have loved you.
John 15:12

Devaluing is the second stage of the abuse cycle. It is made up of actions from the abuser assigning negative qualities to people and disregarding any positive qualities. The idealization stage passes, and the abuser completely focuses on the weaknesses and negative aspects of their target. This is the stage when people notice the mask of the abuser slip and are made to feel extremely unloved, unvaluable, and worthless. However, they continue to stay, hoping to see the abuser revert to the person they were in the beginning.

I felt certain things my abuser did were loving and caring, when they were really acts of abuse and ways of keeping tabs on my whereabouts. Some of these acts were wanting me to FaceTime him when I got home from being with him or him calling me before bed to make sure I was settled in for the night. This allowed him to confirm I was home and in for the night, meaning he didn't have to think about running into me anywhere when he'd go back out for the evening.

Jesus commanded His disciples to love one another in the same way He loves us, as spoken in John 15:12. When people love Jesus, it is reflected in the way they live their daily lives, and others notice they are set apart from the rest of the world. Too often, abuse can be misconstrued as love, especially in the beginning of an abusive cycle when a fast-paced relationship takes shape simultaneously with idealization and love bombing.

When involved in healthy relationships, people will want to love you and find ways to express their love using your love languages (flip back to Day 7 for a list of the love languages). Someone who cares for you will encourage you, push you healthily toward your dreams and goals, and urge you forward by pointing out your positive qualities. They will want to walk beside you and live life with you, adding value to your life the way Jesus added value to the lives of the disciples. But more importantly, they will strive to love you well. Heathy relationships are out there. Keep persevering!

The Garden of Growth
. . . .

 Find today's Scripture in your favorite translation of the Bible (i.e. CSB, NIV, etc.). In your journal, write out the Scripture and reflect on what it means in your life and in your relationships.

Day 16

Term: Baiting
Blessing of Emotions

*A fool gives full vent to his spirit,
but a wise man quietly holds it back.*
Proverbs 29:11

Baiting is a tactic used by abusers to try and provoke an emotional reaction.[8] The abuser usually wants to see negative emotional reactions but will settle for any kind of reaction as long as it provides them with attention to meet their selfish needs.[8] Baiting can also be used to deflect from the abuser's own flaws or mistakes and instead turn the attention to the emotional outburst the abuser is hoping to inflict on the other person.[8]

There was a specific time my abuser did this to me on a Friday afternoon. That weekend, we were supposed to attend a concert I'd purchased tickets for months earlier. Friday morning, he sent me a text message telling me how excited he was to go. A couple hours later, he texted me saying he needed to work over the weekend, implying he wouldn't be able to go to the concert, and he would tell me more about it later. I was extremely frustrated, which resulted in sending him a text message asking him to call me or walk over to my office to sort this out and not wait all day to hear his response. He told me it would have to wait as he didn't have time to step away and talk it through. This created an abundance of confusion and frustration in me, which is what my abuser intended when using baiting.

In hindsight, it was best he didn't call or come to my office to talk because

I'm not certain I could have controlled my emotional reaction. However, it would have been better if he'd waited to tell me when he could make time to talk about the situation rather than creating chaos and me being in an anxious state for the rest of the day.

Proverbs 29:11 clearly tells us we shouldn't let an emotional outburst escape us and instead work on keeping our emotions in check. This isn't to say we are supposed to bottle up our emotions, be robotic, and live life inauthentically. Instead, it would be in our best interest to evaluate the situation and consider what an appropriate response is.

Emotions are a gift from God and He wants us to use our emotions to glorify Him. His intention isn't for us to be controlled by them. God wants us to bring all things to Him, including our emotions, for Him to provide us with the peace and understanding we desire to endure any situation (Philippians 4:6-7). Filling us with His peace is such a loving gesture from a loving God.

The Garden of Growth
• •

Find today's Scripture in your favorite translation of the Bible (i.e. CSB, NIV, etc.). In your journal, write out the Scripture and reflect on what it means in your life and in your relationships.

Day 17

Term: Emotionally Neglectful
God is Near

*When the righteous cry for help, the Lord hears
and delivers them out of all their troubles.
The Lord is near to the brokenhearted
and saves the crushed in spirit.*
Psalm 34:17-18

Being emotionally neglected is painful, especially when the neglect comes from someone who is supposed to love you and care deeply for you. When attempting to make a connection with abusive, emotionally neglectful people, you will find yourself doing most of the strenuous work when it comes to emotional care and response. People who lack emotional intelligence can't build and maintain meaningful connections with others.

My abuser appeared to be emotionally available in the beginning, someone I found to be a safe place to share my dreams, cares, concerns, worries, fears, and goals. I unfortunately learned this was not true, and as our time together progressed, he was most interested in hearing when I was suffering with problems or struggles. He didn't care to hear the good things or celebrate accomplishments with me. It became more noticeable to me as time continued that he was gathering information I shared with him to use it against me later as a way of shaming me or blaming me for something.

I am thankful for Psalm 34:17-18 and how it displays God's loving kindness. Furthermore, it tells us when we call out to God, He listens, cares, is near to us in times of broken heartedness, and saves our crushed spirit. What a relief it is to know the Almighty cares profoundly for us and He is close to us, especially in a time such as this. The Lord doesn't neglect us or our emotions, as does the abusive person, but instead He delivers us from our trouble! The abuser doesn't have the authority to deliver us from our troubles!

As it says in Matthew 7:6, "Do not give dogs what is holy, and do not throw your pearls before pigs, lest they trample them underfoot and turn to attack you." Our innermost thoughts are not meant to be shared with everyone. Unfortunately, I learned this through painful lessons. Not everyone is for us, but God is, and He always wants what is best for us.

The Garden of Growth

 Find today's Scripture in your favorite translation of the Bible (i.e. CSB, NIV, etc.). In your journal, write out the Scripture and reflect on what it means in your life and in your relationships.

Day 18

Term: Silent Treatment
You Do Matter

*For when I kept silent, my bones wasted away
through my groaning all day long.*
Psalm 32:3

The silent treatment is grueling, regardless of who it comes from. It invokes a myriad of emotions, including fear, frustration, anxiety, desperation, or bitterness. The silent treatment is yet another way an abuser attempts to exert control.

For me, this happened often. My abuser would tell me he would call Friday night to make our plans for Saturday. The goal was to make the plan the night before to avoid me waiting for him to call Saturday morning and finding out what time he planned to arrive for our same-day plans. But this typically wouldn't happen. I would sit around waiting for him to call or for him to return my call on Friday night and then I wouldn't hear from him until late Saturday morning or early afternoon. He would say he fell asleep or was on the phone late with family. This was a frequent pattern, and I found out later it wasn't the truth at all. Looking back now, it is apparent he was giving me the silent treatment. He knew I appreciated having plans and knowing how I was going to spend the day and my time, and this was another way for him to be in control in another area of my life.

In Psalm 32:3, David is addressing the physical pain he felt in his body when he sat in silence, not repenting, and not feeling any regret or remorse about his sin. When he held back, didn't repent, and kept it all inside, it turned into physical pain within his own body. While the abuser doesn't necessarily feel pain, remorse, or regret for what they do, others suffer from the silent treatment given by the abuser. The silent treatment makes someone feel disregarded, ignored, ghosted, reduced to second choice, or as if they've been replaced by something better. In a new relationship, it could raise worry or panic thinking something bad happened because of the non-response from the abuser.

The silent treatment is a brutal punishment we don't realize the abuser is using as punishment. The way this inflicts many emotions at once puts our body in overdrive. It isn't your fault if someone used the silent treatment as a way of abuse. I acknowledge this doesn't relieve the pain you feel, but I hope it gives you reassurance and validation you did not deserve it and you did not bring it upon yourself. God is continuing to restore and refine you as you move forward daily, so keep on healing. You are loved.

The Garden of Growth
• •

 Find today's Scripture in your favorite translation of the Bible (i.e. CSB, NIV, etc.). In your journal, write out the Scripture and reflect on what it means in your life and in your relationships.

Day 19

Term: Gaslighting
You're Not Crazy

Do you see a man who is wise in his own eyes?
There is more hope for a fool than for him.
Proverbs 26:12

Have you ever felt the need to record a conversation because you remembered someone saying something, but their past behavior made you doubt they would acknowledge it? If you feel crazy, doubt your recollection of events, or continuously question your reality, there is a high probability you are experiencing gaslighting. Gaslighting is a form of manipulation used when a person attempts to make someone else question their reality, memory of events, or perceptions.[9] "The term 'gaslighting' originates from a 1938 play titled *Gas Light*...[it] follows the story of a husband who manipulates his wife into believing she is losing her mind to control her and gain access to her inheritance."[9]

I recall a time when I asked my abuser where he saw himself in five years, and he gave me a long, drawn-out answer, saying he envisioned us being married for a few years by then. I now know his answer was specifically an example of future faking, but later when I brought it up to him, he said, "Oh, I said that? Hmm, I don't think that's what I said. Maybe you're remembering it wrong." I remember how invalidated I felt, and I wondered why he was denying his statement. Maybe I was hoping this is what he'd said so I made it up in my head or maybe I even dreamed it? Why would he have said it? Did he not really mean it? Am I remembering it wrong? Absolutely not. He said this and he was gaslighting me.

Proverbs 26:12 helps us understand there is no feasible way to have a healthy relationship with a person who views themselves as all-knowing. This is someone who believes their own denial of reality, all things are their way or the highway, and what they say goes because it's always the wisest of all options. I love how the McArthur Study Bible explains this verse: "There are degrees of foolishness, with intellectual conceit being the most stupid and hard to remedy."[10]

As with many things in a relationship with an abuser, gaslighting is yet another way to manipulate and control. However, straight from God's Word, we know this is not someone capable of having a healthy relationship. We should flee from their presence, as they are not teachers of wisdom (Proverbs 14:7). You are a beautiful soul God has intricately created, and no one has the permission to destroy you or take you down. Continue with God by your side every step of the way.

The Garden of Growth

 Find today's Scripture in your favorite translation of the Bible (i.e. CSB, NIV, etc.). In your journal, write out the Scripture and reflect on what it means in your life and in your relationships.

Day 20

Term: Discard
Never Forsaken

"Be strong and courageous. Do not fear or be in dread of them, for it is the Lord your God who goes with you. He will not leave you or forsake you."
Deuteronomy 31:6

The discard is the third stage in the abuse cycle, and it could occur multiple times before a final discard occurs. Abusers discard people for a few reasons: (1) they feel you are too easily manipulated by them and they have begun to look down on you; (2) you are too difficult for them to control; or (3) you are no longer serving their need of ego boosting or helping them reach their goals and they have replaced you with someone else to fulfill their selfish needs. An abuser will not usually discard you until they have secured someone else in your place. My abuser discarded me a handful of times and would re-engage by hoovering (for more on hoovering, see Day 26) to pull me back in and restart the cycle of abuse.

In Deuteronomy 31:6, Moses is telling the people of Israel, God has approved Joshua taking over leading them into the Promised Land and not only is God with them, but He goes before them. The best part of it all is Moses tells them God will never depart from them. This Scripture is very insightful when looking at it in comparison to a relationship with an abusive person. Reflecting on day one of this devotional, when considering how the abuser exhibits a god-like mentality, it again is evident the abuser is truly nothing like God. The abuser discards friends, family, partners—anyone—when they no longer serve a purpose for them. This behavior stands in stark contrast to God, who promises to never leave us nor forsake us! The discard stage can have you feeling lost, as if you're mourning the loss of someone who never actually existed and witnessing someone remove a mask you didn't realize they were wearing. It can cause you to grieve the dreams of a life you thought you were going to have with your "soulmate." Stand firm on the promise of God not leaving or forsaking you, even though your abuser will walk away not giving you a fleeting thought! God will walk beside you through all the emotional turmoil the abuser left behind. He loves you and He cares deeply for His child.

The Garden of Growth

Find today's Scripture in your favorite translation of the Bible (i.e. CSB, NIV, etc.). In your journal, write out the Scripture and reflect on what it means in your life and in your relationships.

Day 21

Term: Denial
God's Protection

*Jesus said to him, "Truly, I tell you, this very night, before
the rooster crows, you will deny me three times." Peter
said to him, "Even if I must die with you, I will not deny
you!" And all the disciples said the same.*
Matthew 26:34-35

When disconnecting from an abusive person, it is expected you will go through stages of grief (denial, anger, bargaining, depression, and acceptance), with denial being the first stage. You want to believe the person you knew was the kind, loving, caring person and not the maskless, emotionless person who emerged when you cut them off for the final time.

The first overwhelming sense of denial I felt after leaving my abuser the final time came when I pulled a background check that encompassed an expunged criminal record for Felony Battery, Domestic Battery by Strangulation. Seeing this was shocking to me as I'd never witnessed him being violent, and I felt there was no way this information was correct for the person I thought I knew. I required time to process the information to move through the denial.

In Matthew 26:30-35, Jesus is breaking bread at the Last Supper with His disciples, and Jesus explains one of them is going to deny Him three times before the next morning. Of Jesus' disciples, Peter, James, and John were the closest with Jesus. The three of them accompanied Jesus on the

Mount of Transfiguration (Matthew 17:1-8). Peter is adamant he will not deny Christ. When Peter heard Jesus say a disciple was going to deny Him, it didn't cross Peter's mind he would be the denying disciple. Later, in Matthew 26:69-75, Peter denies Christ three times as Jesus foretold. But if we flip to Luke 22:61-62, this adds an extra detail about when Peter made his third and final denial of knowing Jesus. The rooster crowed while he was still talking, Jesus made eye contact with him, and Peter immediately remembered what Jesus foretold. Then, Peter left and wept bitterly. The eye contact brought to light the realization Peter had at that very moment.

When we separate from our abuser, our mind starts to clear, and the haze starts to lift. We begin to see more clearly and understand the abuse we lived through, but we also remember good times, and denial arises. We even wonder if we should give it another chance. It's best not to go back. Long term, the relationship won't be any different. This is the cycle in abusive relationships—abusers don't abuse 100 percent of the time, and there are good times of feeling genuine love sprinkled in with the abusive behaviors.

When experiencing the denial accompanied by emotional abuse, the first thing to do is accept who the abuser reveals themselves to be. The abuser fully reveals their true colors at the end of a relationship and it's who they've always been. As hard as it is to wrap our minds around it, we must accept it, process it, and move through it. This is who they are, and we deserve more than what they have given us. It is in our best interest to move forward, rid ourselves of the haze blocking our view of the truth, and rely on God to continue revealing the truth, as hard as it may be. By God revealing these truths and lifting the fog, He is protecting us from going back to something unhealthy. And imagine—we can't even dream what God has in store for us. Whatever we are dreaming for ourselves, God's plans for us are bigger. Keep relying on God to bring forth the truth and reveal where you need to have closure and heal.

The Garden of Growth

• •

Find today's Scripture in your favorite translation of the Bible (i.e. CSB, NIV, etc.). In your journal, write out the Scripture and reflect on what it means in your life and in your relationships.

Day 22

Term: Victim Blaming
Mercy Triumphs

For judgment is without mercy to one who has shown no mercy. Mercy triumphs over judgment.
James 2:13

Leaving an abusive relationship is difficult, but the victim blaming frequently following can add significantly to the overall pain and is hard to comprehend. Victim blaming is when the fault of abuse or trauma is placed on the person who underwent the abuse (the survivor) instead of the person who carried out the abuse (the abuser). This can feel complicated if the victim blaming comes from someone close to us or someone we felt was trustworthy and safe.

When I left, I shared my story with a person I considered a friend, who knew my abuser, and she said, "Well, he has never been those ways with me. I'm not going to stop talking to him or stop being friends with him because he's never done anything to me." I remember how awful I felt because it seemed like she was blaming me for the abuse I innocently suffered because of his actions. I chose to no longer speak to her after our conversation ended because I didn't want to associate with someone who knew about the abuse and was still willing to include him as part of her life. All I thought was she could be his next victim if she wasn't careful and didn't heed the warnings.

James 2:13 explains it is necessary to show mercy and compassion to others so God will be merciful to us on the day of judgement. While people place the blame on the victim, God doesn't. I say this with the story of the Woman at the Well in mind from John 4. She was collecting water from the well, and Jesus was passing by and asked for a drink of water. As they began talking, Jesus told her He knew she was married five times and the man she was living with was not her husband. As the story continues, it is apparent others blamed her for multiple marriages and cohabitating with a man outside of marriage. However, Jesus didn't place blame on her. In this time, it was not unusual to be married multiple times, as women married at a young age and were often widowed because of marrying much older men due to the culture of arranged marriages. It also wasn't unusual to cohabitate with a man a woman wasn't married to as the woman could have been a concubine. [11]

God has considerably better for you, my sweet friend. He is a loving, merciful God and will make a way forward. I encourage you to read John 4:1-45 for the full story of this woman, how she was personally changed, and the way she encouraged others from the conversation she unexpectedly shared with Jesus at the well. You're twenty-two days into moving forward to the beautiful life God has ahead for you.

The Garden of Growth
• •

 Find today's Scripture in your favorite translation of the Bible (i.e. CSB, NIV, etc.). In your journal, write out the Scripture and reflect on what it means in your life and in your relationships.

Day 23

Term: Trauma Bond
Keep Good Company

Do not be deceived: "Bad company ruins good morals."
1 Corinthians 15:33

A trauma bond is a deep connection developed over time from the cycle of abuse (physical and/or emotional) occurring repeatedly. It can develop over weeks, months, or years of repeated abuse and each person facing this has their own unique trauma. The good news is not everyone who has been in an abusive relationship develops a trauma bond.

Before I met my abuser and in the beginning of our relationship, I was a happy, bubbly, and positive person. However, the longer we were together, the more trauma bonded I became to him, and I quickly became a shell of who I once was. I became unrecognizable to myself. I didn't realize it then, but in hindsight, I was no longer fun to be around. I was usually in pain with an autoimmune flare-up or a horrible headache, crying, complaining, and plain miserable. I thought there was something inherently wrong with me, and I did what I could to improve upon myself, which I hoped would improve our relationship. My friends and my mom were exceptionally patient with me. They listened to me and offered me advice and their shoulders to cry on while I suffered through not understanding the depths of what I was enduring.

An abuser is not a person who anyone with good morals should choose to associate with, and a trauma bond encourages it—a trauma bond entangles people together with cycle and repetition. First Corinthians 15:33 points out spending time with those with bad intentions, morals, or values will corrupt any good parts in someone. It is similar to the saying, "you are the company you keep." I learned how our emotional pain can reveal itself as physical pain and chronic illness within our bodies. There is a holistic technique my chiropractor performed on me called the Neuro Emotional Technique (NET), using a muscle test to identify and release stuck emotions causing me physical pain. During my healing, it helped to identify emotions I had so I could determine the best way to process them, how they were tied to my relationship, and break free of the negative effects they were having on my overall life.

Someone who loves and cares for you will not have to manipulate you or cause you to become emotionally stuck to remain in the relationship. They will not put you through abuse and get you unhealthily attached to them where the chaos and pain feels normal. If you felt this, you aren't alone. Chaos feels normal in abusive relationships. Safely disengaging is the best option to regain your self-worth, self-confidence, power, strength, and personality. God promises your lost years will be restored (Joel 2:25-26).

The Garden of Growth
• •

Find today's Scripture in your favorite translation of the Bible (i.e. CSB, NIV, etc.). In your journal, write out the Scripture and reflect on what it means in your life and in your relationships.

Day 24

Term: Complex Post Traumatic Stress Disorder (CPTSD)
God Fights for You

*For we do not wrestle against flesh and blood, but against
the rulers, against the authorities, against the cosmic
powers over this present darkness, against the spiritual
forces of evil in the heavenly places.*
Ephesians 6:12

Complex Post Traumatic Stress Disorder (CPTSD) is similar to Post Traumatic Stress Disorder (PTSD) but more complicated to live with every day. It shows up with all the symptoms of PTSD plus additional symptoms, such as lack of emotional regulation and hypervigilance (for more on hypervigilance, see Day 28). It is different from PTSD, as PTSD results from experiencing a single traumatic event, whereas CPTSD results from experiencing abuse for extended periods of time.[12]

In August 2022, when I was diagnosed with CPTSD, among other diagnosis that arose from the abuse I'd endured, I felt a deep sense of loneliness, and darkness came over me. As I took the time to accept the diagnosis, familiarize myself with what I'd encountered, and how it affected me, it gave me comfort knowing there was a name for it—for my sometimes-uncontrollable crying spells and for my severe hypervigilance. I was thankful I possessed the financial means to receive a diagnosis because it helped me in moving forward, learning how to live everyday life and how to cope with what my body was feeling.

While fighting CPTSD is an earthly battle, it is also a spiritual battle. In this world we encounter battles not against flesh and blood but against Satan and his demons. These adversaries scheme things against us and attack us using our weaknesses, including our trauma after an abusive relationship. Ephesians 6:12 helps us to understand the existence of a real spiritual realm—the devil and his demons want to try and remove us from the presence of God and send us into the deepest pits of darkness.

It is important for you to know a diagnosis is not your identity, although it is part of your story. When you feel darkness coming over you, hold tight to God who is right beside you and ready to fight any battles against the spiritual realm for you. Turn your eyes to Jesus, call out to Him to draw near, rely on Him, and pray against any feelings of darkness or defeat. Tirelessly run to Him and trust in Him to protect you from the evil surrounding us in this world, especially from the spiritual realm.

The Garden of Growth

Find today's Scripture in your favorite translation of the Bible (i.e. CSB, NIV, etc.). In your journal, write out the Scripture and reflect on what it means in your life and in your relationships.

Day 25

Term: Dissociation
Rely on God

For we do not want you to be unaware, brothers, of the affliction we experienced in Asia. For we were so utterly burdened beyond our strength that we despaired of life itself. Indeed, we felt that we had received the sentence of death. But that was to make us rely not on ourselves but on God who raises the dead. He delivered us from such a deadly peril, and he will deliver us. On him we have set our hope that he will deliver us again.
2 Corinthians 1:8-10

"The term dissociation is used for describing our natural human ability to move mentally away from immediate surroundings and 'lose ourselves' in something else."[13] Dissociation can manifest as keeping ourselves excessively occupied with various activities to avoid thoughts of the abuse endured, constantly seeking background noise like TV, podcasts, or music because silence is distressing, or resorting to addictive behaviors such as substance use to numb our thoughts. I dealt with dissociation often after leaving, and even for longer than I expected at the beginning of my healing journey. I felt as though I was detached from my body, observing my life unfold as if from a distance. It seemed like an out of body experience and once I would come back to reality, it would take me a few minutes to shake off the feeling and regain my composure. I could not sit down on the couch to relax, and I chose to keep myself busy doing something around the house because if I sat down, I would cry uncontrollably, and it was difficult for me to stop and regulate my nervous system.

Paul is addressing the church of Corinth in 2 Corinthians 1:8-10. He is telling about a distressing situation he underwent in Asia as he was spreading the gospel. While the details of the event are not known, it is clear from these verses Paul went through something he didn't think he would live to tell about, and he thought it was going to end his ministry. These circumstances were horrific and there was nothing humanly possible Paul could have leaned on to help him survive, not even to dissociate. So, he knew he required full reliance on God to rescue him. Paul put all his hope in God, and He rescued Paul from a death sentence.

I understand the time it takes to heal after the relationship ends may feel infinite but keep relying on God to walk with you. During times of dissociation, He will prove tenfold the hope He gives to the hopeless, rest for the weary, and love for the broken heart. He is right beside you.

The Garden of Growth

 Find today's Scripture in your favorite translation of the Bible (i.e. CSB, NIV, etc.). In your journal, write out the Scripture and reflect on what it means in your life and in your relationships.

Day 26

Term: Hoovering
Abundant Life

The thief comes only to steal and kill and destroy. I came that they may have life and have it abundantly.
John 10:10

Hoovering is the fourth stage of the abuse cycle occurring after the abuser completes the discard. The abuser comes back around and works to pull the person back into a relationship with them. This could happen days, weeks, months, or even years after the discard. This may occur by the abuser sending a birthday text message, calling to see how you're doing, or something even more, such as sending flowers or buying a nice gift and groveling with apologies.

As mentioned previously, I was hoovered by my abuser and returned to him a total of five times before I left for good. Each time I went back, the emotional abuse was worse and the time between each discard and hoover became shorter. Each time I went back, I was hopeful it would be different and it wouldn't be a repeat of what had happened each time before. I'm immensely grateful God gave me the strength to walk away for the final time.

When the abuser hoovers, it resembles the thief mentioned in John 10:10. When they attempt to re-engage with you, they aim to steal your joy, kill your happiness, and bring destruction to your life as they did before. According to the National Domestic Violence Hotline, survivors return to their abusers an average of seven times before they leave for good. [14] Each time a return to the relationship takes place, the abuse doesn't disappear—it gets worse. Avoid re-engaging at all costs.

I wholeheartedly want you to know you are meant for more. We are meant to live a life God has designed especially for us, and it doesn't involve living in continual abuse. God created us to live out an abundant life built of rich moments with our loved ones, both family and friends. He created us to be open and willing to live out His will for our lives. You were made on purpose *for* a purpose, and the fact you are reading this book shows God is not done with you yet! Allow God to work through you to give you the most bountiful life.

The Garden of Growth

Find today's Scripture in your favorite translation of the Bible (i.e. CSB, NIV, etc.). In your journal, write out the Scripture and reflect on what it means in your life and in your relationships.

Day 27

Term: Cognitive Dissonance/Double Mindedness
The Mind of God

*I hate the double-minded,
but I love your law.*
Psalm 119:113

Cognitive dissonance is when two contradictory views are thought at the same time. It literally means inharmonious thought.[15] Double mindedness is when you know the truth but are choosing to have an opposing thought. This happens in abusive relationships because abusers aren't bad and abusive 100 percent of the time. When in a relationship with someone who emotionally abuses, manipulates, and gaslights you, they will do something kind and caring from time to time to provide you with breadcrumbs of attention to keep you hanging on. It makes it difficult to believe the person's true self is more aligned with abuser traits, which reflect who they really are.

The way things ended with my abuser exposed qualities about him I'd never witnessed before. He was furious I confronted him with the information I'd found and he yelled at me. Until then, he had never yelled or raised his voice at me. Moreover, we were on FaceTime and he hung up on me. There was no way this was the same person I'd dated for almost three years of my life. He immediately became a stranger to me, but I thought maybe he was having a bad day already and I'd made it worse, because the person who yelled at me was not the person I knew. These inharmonious thoughts were confusing and frustrating as I tried to make sense of who he really was.

In Psalm 119:113, cognitive dissonance is referred to as double mindedness. In Romans 7:22-25, Paul was succumbing to the flesh/human nature as we all do. Because of our humanness, we all wrestle with the Holy Spirit inside of us and keeping God's law perfectly.[16] We are all working to be at peace with ourselves, and the more God renews our minds, the closer we will become to fulfilling the deep desire for inner peace and limiting the spiritual war we wage inside.

Despite the difficulty, my abuser felt like a stranger to me. If you're struggling with this, it's time to accept what you've been shown. There's nothing you did to make it happen and there's nothing you can do to make them change. It doesn't fall on your shoulders and it's not your responsibility to change them. Someone can decide to genuinely change once they are prepared to take full accountability for their actions and the harm they caused. Keep going! You're not far from experiencing beauty on the other side of this tragic heartbreak.

The Garden of Growth

 Find today's Scripture in your favorite translation of the Bible (i.e. CSB, NIV, etc.). In your journal, write out the Scripture and reflect on what it means in your life and in your relationships.

Day 28

Term: Hypervigilance
No Fear in Love

There is no fear in love, but perfect love casts out fear. For fear has to do with punishment, and whoever fears has not been perfected in love.
1 John 4:18

Hypervigilance is the constant state of being afraid. This shows up as continually being on the lookout for potential threats. It's more than being aware of your surroundings, which is a normal level of awareness; hypervigilance is a few notches above this.

While leaving my abuser was the best decision to take care of myself physically, mentally, and spiritually, I did feel severe hypervigilance. If I spent time out with friends, I asked them to come to my house or at least to my side of town to meet for dinner because I didn't want to run into him somewhere. Because of the way things had ended and what I'd witnessed when we broke up for the final time, I didn't know how things would go if I ran into him in public. I was constantly on alert, wide-eyed, and my head was on a swivel. There was a period when I was legitimately concerned for my safety.

God is not a God of fear and because hypervigilance is rooted in fear, the relationship with the abuser was not a gift from God and not one He hopes we remain in. There is much to unpack in 1 John 4:18. I appreciate the Scripture pointing out fear has to do with punishment and love casts out fear. This means if you fear your abuser, it's impossible for love to exist, for whoever fears has not been perfected in love. Wow. What a powerful statement. Someone cannot both love *and* inflict fear.

The one and only true God loves you, and you don't have to be fearful of Him coming to harm you for He wants good for your life! His love is perfect! When you feel periods of hypervigilance, close your eyes and think of your loving heavenly Father wrapping you in a huge hug and protecting you from all potential danger. This is true love casting out all fear. If you can take a moment to breathe and imagine this beautiful picture, you can be sure you are well on your way to healing!

The Garden of Growth

Find today's Scripture in your favorite translation of the Bible (i.e. CSB, NIV, etc.). In your journal, write out the Scripture and reflect on what it means in your life and in your relationships.

Day 29

Term: Fauxpology
God Meant Good

As for you, you meant evil against me, but God meant it for good, to bring it about that many people should be kept alive, as they are today.
Genesis 50:20

Fauxpology is exactly as it sounds: a fake apology made by an abuser that often mimics a genuine apology but avoids accepting responsibility for their actions. It may come across as, "I'm sorry you got mad because of what I said" or "I'm sorry you are always so sensitive about everything." It's not an actual apology asking for forgiveness for hurting you but instead one saying the empty words of "I'm sorry" and deflecting the blame onto someone else for the damage done.

When my abuser arrived late to my house for dates, each time he would apologize profusely. I expressed to him how frustrating it was to me and how I would appreciate him making more of an effort to be on time, but under no circumstances did his behavior change. He continued to be hours late and not be respectful of my time. This was something I eventually overlooked, and his apologies became empty words.

In Genesis 50:15-21, when Joseph's brothers found out their father had passed away, they feared Joseph's retaliation since they'd sold him into slavery. His brothers used the words, "I'm sorry," but it came across as a fauxpology, said solely to avoid retaliation from Joseph.[17] In Genesis 50:17, Joseph wept when they apologized to him, but I don't feel he wept out of gratitude for their apology, I feel he wept because he didn't believe they were genuinely apologizing for their evil acts and the pain they'd caused Joseph for years on end. When an abuser apologizes, it feels altogether disingenuous, as though they are only checking it off a list or trying to save themselves from facing consequences.

The best part of this story with Joseph and his brothers is how Joseph responded to them in Genesis 50:20, telling them they'd desired evil for him but God meant it all for good! While his brothers were shaking in their boots afraid of Joseph's revenge, Joseph let them know they couldn't supersede the Lord and what He divinely intended for his life. Just as with you, the abuser wanted to take you down and gave you fake apologies along the way, but God has delivered you and brought you out safely for a better life!

The Garden of Growth
. . . .

Find today's Scripture in your favorite translation of the Bible (i.e. CSB, NIV, etc.). In your journal, write out the Scripture and reflect on what it means in your life and in your relationships.

Day 30

Term: Smear Campaign
God's Vengeance

*You shall be hidden from the lash of the tongue,
and shall not fear destruction when it comes.*
Job 5:21

The smear campaign is a tactic the abuser will use to try to ruin your reputation. This doesn't have to be enacted at the conclusion of a relationship—the abuser can do this throughout by feeding stories and lies about you to mutual acquaintances. This sets up the perfect scenario for when everything comes crashing down—people assume the abuser had nothing to do with the fallout. The abuser can then play the victim role and get sympathy from the lies they had previously spread. This may involve them lying about how they were treated, saying they were cheated on, or completely dismantling the other person's character.

Job 5:21 is part of an encouraging conversation between Job and his friend Eliphaz, where Eliphaz explains to Job how God will protect him from all destruction, including when others talk negatively about him. The Scripture reveals how God hides us from the enemy, their schemes, and any destruction they intend to cause us.

Please understand it's not relevant what others say about you—it only matters what God says about you. And He says you are:

- Fearfully and wonderfully made – Psalm 139:34
- Chosen – John 15:16
- His child – John 1:12
- Free – Romans 8:2, Galatians 5:1
- A new creation – 2 Corinthians 5:17
- His friend – John 15:15
- Justified – Romans 3:24
- Redeemed – Romans 6:6
- Victorious – Romans 8:37

I'm fiercely proud of you! You made it through the thirty days of Truth through Understanding! I hope your faith was deepened and you see truth straight from God's Word filling your life.

The Garden of Growth

Find today's Scripture in your favorite translation of the Bible (i.e. CSB, NIV, etc.). In your journal, write out the Scripture and reflect on what it means in your life and in your relationships.

Section Two
Truth through Prayer

Likewise the Spirit helps us in our weakness. For we do not know what to pray for as we ought, but the Spirit himself intercedes for us with groanings too deep for words.
Romans 8:26

I was distraught when I walked away from my relationship. I was a ball of emotions, and I wasn't sure what to pray or even how to come to the feet of Jesus in this situation. Should I be praying for restoration, praying for the Lord to forgive me for ignoring the signs He provided, or praying the Lord would help me to forgive my abuser? Some days, I felt angry and I didn't want to pray, and some days, I was emotionally and mentally drained, I couldn't compile any words to form a prayer. Many times, I simply spoke the name *Jesus* and cried. I knew He still heard my groans and He knew my pain. In fact, He sat with me through it all because He is moved by our grief.

Psychologist and author, Diane Langberg, Ph.D. spoke on Isaiah 45:2-3 at the 2022 Restore Conference.[18] The Scripture says,

> *"I will go before you
> and level the exalted places,
> I will break in pieces the doors of bronze
> and cut through the bars of iron,
> I will give you the treasures of darkness*

> *and the hoards in secret places,*
> *that you may know that it is I, the Lord,*
> *the God of Israel, who call you by your name."*

To summarize Dr. Langberg's teaching, God, the treasure in the darkness, gives us hope during seasons of pain and suffering. He gives us hope so we know who He is, and we understand He is the one who has the power to intervene on our behalf. He calls us by name for our identity in Christ to be clear—we are who He says we are, which is a beloved child of our heavenly Father. Furthermore, during a conversation with Karen DeArmond Gardner, author of *Hope for Healing from Domestic Abuse,* she expanded on Dr. Langberg's teaching explaining how we can dwell in the presence of God, known as the secret place, for as long as we need. As He sits with us in darkness and grief, we discover the richness of God. He peels away what we thought we believed about Him and shows us His true character, how He is for the vulnerable, and how much He loves us and cares about our suffering. He wants to sit with us in those deep, dark places. God doesn't *only* want us to pray to Him, He wants us to have encounters with Him!

Section Two will provide you with thirty days of prayers to move you forward on the path of healing. Utilize these prayers when you don't have the words to pray or the strength to form coherent sentences. You may want to return to these multiple times throughout your healing. And don't feel bad if you pray and then sit in silence. God speaks in times of silence; therefore, allow Him time to speak into your life and be open to having encounters with Jesus.

Day 31
Break Free

But he turned and said to Peter, "Get behind me, Satan! You are a hindrance to me. For you are not setting your mind on the things of God, but on the things of man."
Matthew 16:23

Initially, one of the hardest parts of starting to heal was implementing the no-contact rule when everything collapsed. No contact means deleting/blocking your abuser from social media, not talking to their family, and, generally, not communicating with them. In fact, blocking and deleting their number would be the best course of action. There were days it was painfully difficult not to call or text my abuser. Communicating with him had become part of my everyday life and was a habit I desired to break. Thankfully, when I was tempted to reach out to him, I called or texted friends or my mom to fill the void. As time progressed, I started praying to fill the void instead. I understand not everyone can abstain from contact depending on your personal situation (i.e., having children together), but this step is crucial to healing. Some ideas to help minimize communication are having a family member do child drop offs on your behalf. This prevents you having to engage in person. Another option is to communicate via email when it is necessary to discuss something. Communicating this way provides an electronic record, but it also allows the point to be stated without becoming stuck on a phone call for hours on end. If these aren't viable options, I suggest calling the 24/7 National Domestic Violence Hotline (1-800-799-

7233) and asking for guidance and resources for how to minimize contact. Remaining in limited and necessary contact does not mean you cannot heal or it's hopeless to live a beautiful and safe life. Don't feel discouraged. There are resources and ways to do this safely.

When you have determined the relationship is over and you are ready to take your life back, it's time to have no contact. The times you feel tempted to contact your abuser, I hope you will say this prayer to give you strength to avoid sending a text or hitting the "call" button.

Almighty God,
In this moment, I am tempted and weak and lift my prayer to You. I know communicating with my abuser doesn't benefit me in a positive way. You know interacting with them became part of my daily routine and it formed a habit I need to break. I ask right now for strength to not contact them and to focus on my bond with You. I ask You to fill any void I have. I know You love me unconditionally and want what's best for me, and that relationship is not Your best for my life. I pray for courage to stand strong in the face of temptation and in moments of weakness. I believe I can lean on Your everlasting arms to hold me upright and not fall into temptation and allow my abuser access into my life again.
I pray in Your name, Amen.

The Garden of Growth

When you feel tempted to contact your abuser, who are some friends or family you can contact instead?

Did God reveal anything during or after your prayer? If so, what?

Day 32
You're Not a Burden

*Two are better than one, because they have a good
reward for their toil. For if they fall, one will lift up his
fellow. But woe to him who is alone when he falls and has
not another to lift him up!*
Ecclesiastes 4:9-10

I struggled with feeling as though I was a constant burden to my abuser. I often felt I asked for too much when I wanted to spend more than one day a week together or to have a conversation over the phone or FaceTime when we weren't spending as much time together. I was told by friends and family I wasn't asking for too much and I wasn't asking for anything another person in my position wouldn't also desire. I found myself thanking my abuser when we spent time together, as if it was an extreme honor to be together and as though he'd made a sacrifice to spend time with me. This caused me to persistently feel I was an annoyance to him.

When we are constantly surrounded by this message, it can easily carry over into other areas of our lives, such as with friends, family, or colleagues. Let me assure you, you are not a burden, and what you have to say is valuable. Your needs matter, too. Relationships should not bog us down but instead lift us up. They should be comprised of give and take, not single sided. It is important to know God made you and considers you His masterpiece. I encourage you to pray this prayer when you feel you are asking for too much, pushing down your desires to speak up, not requesting what you need, or not asking for help in fear of being a burden to someone.

Heavenly Father,
You are profoundly good to me, and You created me as Your masterpiece. This is something incredibly beautiful to reflect on. I know You created me for relationships and connection with others. Your Word is clear: I am to help carry the burdens of others and I should lift others up. Help me to remember I can ask for the same. Guide me to reach out for support when I need it and be open to receiving help from others. May I find peace in knowing You placed people in my life who care for me and want to share in my burdens. Give me reminders that I am not a burden and I am not asking for too much.
I pray in Your name, Amen.

The Garden of Growth
• •

What are ways you can remind yourself you aren't a burden and what you are asking for isn't too much?

Did God reveal anything during or after your prayer? If so, what?

Day 33
Be Patient with Yourself

And we urge you, brothers, admonish the idle, encourage the fainthearted, help the weak, be patient with them all.
1 Thessalonians 5:14

Healing from the effects of abuse is not an overnight undertaking. It may be accompanied by a rollercoaster of emotions. Some days I felt great—happy and light—and other days I was crying, couldn't pull myself out of bed, and felt myself sinking into a dark hole. While it didn't feel like an actual part of the "normal" healing process, I learned it was. Healing is not a linear process. It takes time for progress to become evident and positive emotions to radiate when healing from emotional abuse. I gave myself permission to feel each emotion and I learned to be patient with myself as my nervous system worked at returning to a restful state of being and I learned to regulate my emotions in a healthy way. In 1 Thessalonians, Paul is talking about how pastors are to serve people and how the people are to respond. The way Paul describes how to handle each type of person isn't just about how we should treat *others*, but it is also about how we should treat ourselves, as it says to "be patient with them all"–the "them all" piece of the Scripture includes ourselves.

Recognizing and admitting to myself healing would take more time than I anticipated was a huge step. Learning to be kind to myself as I worked through the process was an even bigger step. As you work through your own journey of healing and learn to show patience and kindness to yourself, say the following prayer and return to it as many times as you need to help with moving towards the rebuilding of your life.

Dear Lord,
I come humbly before You today, asking for Your help in granting me patience for myself. I can easily find patience for others going through difficult times, but I can't always show myself the same compassion. Please help me to acknowledge my healing isn't going to happen overnight. When I'm being hard on myself or feeling frustrated and I can't just "get over it," please give me a gentle reminder in Your loving way that I will get there with Your help, in Your time, and to be patient with myself and the process of healing.
I pray in Your name, Amen.

The Garden of Growth
• •

 What are specific ways you can practice patience with yourself?

 Did God reveal anything during or after your prayer? If so, what?

Day 34
Be Patient with God

...but they who wait for the Lord shall renew their strength;
they shall mount up with wings like eagles;
they shall run and not be weary;
they shall walk and not faint.
Isaiah 40:31

Although I felt weak, weary, and shattered, God walked beside me in my heartbreak and grief. There were days I couldn't bring myself to get out of bed because of the physical pain I felt in my chest, and I wondered if I was experiencing true heartbreak. I knew God didn't cause my pain, but it was hard for me to understand how there wasn't another way He could have rescued me from my situation. Then I realized: He lovingly gave me several signs, some through dreams, which could have minimized the time spent in my relationship, but I didn't heed the warnings. It was because of my humanness I stayed with someone who was very hurtful. As I continued to walk through the journey of healing, I relied on the Lord more every day than ever before, and I started to feel strengthened and stronger each day. I found my strength in the Lord, and I allowed Him to guide me and give me His next steps all along the way. I was spending time with God in new ways and expressing gratitude for the smallest things in life. I learned through my own healing if I stick close to God, He will carry me when things get too heavy. He renewed me and strengthened me, and I know He will do the same for you! Pray this prayer when the load feels heavy and you need God's strength.

Dear Lord,
You are a way maker and every day You show me Your ways and how deeply You love me. It is hard to have patience in healing when the pain is so deep, and it's easy to want to take things under my own control time and time again. Lord, I lay this situation at Your feet today and ask for You to reveal all things in Your time. Help me to be patient in Your plan for my life and not try to control every step of the way but rely on faith and know You are constantly watching over me and want what's best for my life. I love You and I'm grateful.
I pray in Your name, Amen.

The Garden of Growth
• •

What are specific ways you can practice patience with God?

Did God reveal anything during or after your prayer? If so, what?

Day 35
Healing Takes Time

Many are the afflictions of the righteous,
but the Lord delivers him out of them all.
He keeps all his bones;
not one of them is broken.
Psalm 34:19-20

Healing is a process. It doesn't happen overnight and there isn't a specific timeline. Every person is different in how long it takes, whether it be healing physically, emotionally, mentally, spiritually, or financially. It is a roller coaster, which is a reason some people choose not to do the work. Healing is messy, but it is worth the time and the effort in the long run. Healing allows you to live a full life, find your joy, and live your God-given purpose.

As you heal, it could open other areas in your life you need to address. I highly encourage you to recognize and focus on any areas as you are ready because it's all part of the larger picture! I don't regret allowing myself space to heal from the other tough things brought forth. I encourage you to give yourself grace and understanding and realize healing takes time. Don't get discouraged if you feel you took five steps forward followed by two steps back. You're still ahead. You will get there. Keep pressing forward, persevering, and looking forward to one day sharing your testimony of what God brought you through. To summarize the words from a conversation with Karen DeArmond Gardner, author of *Hope for Healing from Domestic Abuse*, the ashes in Isaiah 61:3 don't represent all the ugly we went through—the ashes represent the healing we did because it's hard, challenging, and messy. God turns those ashes into a beautiful headdress for us to wear. What amazing insight! Pray this prayer when you need assurance there isn't a timeline to heal from what you went through and to remember God is working on your beautiful crown.

Dear Lord,
Healing feels like a roller coaster. Sometimes the healing is more painful than what I'm working to heal from. I pray You help me to find comfort in knowing there is no timeline for how long it will take and You will restore me wholly and to what You intend for my life. Even though healing feels lonely at times, help me to remember it won't be this way forever. I ask You to bring beauty from ashes and joy in the morning. Great is Your faithfulness, God!
I pray in Your name, Amen.

The Garden of Growth

Thinking about your healing journey so far, acknowledge a few steps you have taken towards healing.

Did God reveal anything during or after your prayer? If so, what?

Day 36
Daily Motivation

Whatever you do, work heartily, as for the Lord and not for men.
Colossians 3:23

The lack of motivation feels excessive at times when healing from emotional abuse. Trying to accept the truth while also trying to take care of ourselves and live our daily lives can feel extremely overwhelming. Something to remember, sweet friend, is if you wake up feeling 40 percent out of 100 percent but you give 100 percent of your 40 percent, then you're giving all you can. Some days, you will give the bare minimum of getting out of bed, showering, going to work, and going to bed. Other days, it will be more. It is essential to your healing to listen to what your body needs. Lean on God because all you do in life is for His glory. You are working to please Him and Him alone. God wants us to take care of the bodies He gave us, so be sure you are getting proper rest, eating well, and allowing God to walk alongside you daily. Pray this prayer asking God to spur you on when motivation seems difficult. He will do it!

*Dear Lord,
It isn't easy for me to get out of bed and push myself to make it through the day. Sometimes, the lack of motivation is more than I can bear and I want to stay in bed and sleep all day because then I don't have to face reality. I understand there are days I need to, but I cannot let it become a daily occurrence. I pray You will*

walk beside me on the days I feel defeated with no motivation to do even the simplest tasks. I pray I would feel Your love and encouragement and You would help me persevere with Your strength. I ask every day You would help me to feel stronger and more motivated to push through life's difficulties with You by my side. I love You, Lord, and thank You for Your companionship and friendship during this difficult time.
I pray in Your name, Amen.

The Garden of Growth

What percentage of motivation have you felt lately? On days you are feeling low motivation, how do you cope with the struggle? What are specific tools you use to get you out of the rut?

Did God reveal anything during or after your prayer? If so, what?

Day 37
Grief Isn't Linear

... a time to weep, and a time to laugh;
a time to mourn, and a time to dance;
Ecclesiastes 3:4

Grief. There is a copious amount of information people don't talk about when it comes to grieving. Something I learned was grieving accompanied with healing was one of the loneliest times in my life. I felt stuck in constant grief—I didn't know how to bring myself out of it, and it appeared everyone was moving forward normally with their own lives. I yearned for the grieving to end as fast as possible, but I knew I needed to allow myself to grieve, as grieving is part of healing. I desperately wanted to move forward and figure out how to live a life full of laughter and joy again. Also, I lost count of how many times I told myself grieving, the same as healing, isn't linear. Some days I felt totally fine and then a memory, a smell, or a song brought all the feelings rushing back to the surface. When this happened, I felt I wasn't moving forward, but I was. Any time something resembling this occurs, embrace moving through it rather than past it or over it.

God reminds us in His Word there is a time to weep and mourn, but then there is also a time to laugh and dance. I noticed as I read this Scripture we weep, then we laugh, then we mourn, and then we dance. This Scripture alone makes it clear to me healing and grief are not linear. You may sense you're in a long, dark, endless tunnel, but be encouraged because there is light ahead! Pray this prayer when you don't feel like you're seeing the light and need a reminder it's there.

Dear Lord,
There are days when I feel I'm in a dark tunnel. Some days I feel improvement to my mental health and then other days I feel I'm taking steps backwards and don't feel I'm headed in the direction of healing at all. Your Word reminds me there is a time for everything under the sun, so I pray I would see the light more clearly in times of darkness or defeat and find solace in the promises from Your Word. Help me to remember grief isn't linear, but we also don't have to walk through it alone. Just as You are the Light of the World, I pray You will be the light in my darkness and bring all this to pass.
I pray in Your name, Amen.

The Garden of Growth
• •

 How does it feel to sit in grief? Is it uncomfortable? Sad? Empowering you can hold space for yourself? Heavy? Describe it in as much detail as possible.

 Did God reveal anything during or after your prayer? If so, what?

Day 38
Be Present

*"Be still, and know that I am God.
I will be exalted among the nations,
I will be exalted in the earth!"*
Psalm 46:10

I dissociated often as I was on my path to healing. There are many ways to dissociate, such as absent-mindedly scrolling social media or watching a familiar show to avoid sitting in silence. These activities typically cause someone to "zone out" and not deal with the current situation. When we are used to being in a constant state of chaos, sitting still and reflecting quietly feels strange, uncomfortable, and sometimes even wrong. But the more we can sit, reflect, be still, and be present, the more peace we find within. We can find peace with God in those quiet moments.

Sometimes these moments came when walking my dogs before the sun came up. Sometimes I would sit on the couch and drink my coffee with a soft light on, taking in the smell of the coffee or the candle I was burning. The more I did these types of things, the more I realized I was taking care of my soul. I was still and opening my heart to hear what God wanted to say to me. I was quieting all the noise around me and allowing God to be God and speak into my life. On August 13, 2021, I was in the shower, and I was crying, like big-time sobbing. God spoke to me and said, "It's okay, my daughter. I'm right here holding you close. You will be okay. I promised to never leave you and I'm still right here." I encourage you to be still, but present, and open your heart to hear from God when He speaks the way He spoke to me in August 2021. Pray this prayer when you need to be still and present and open your heart to what God wants to show you.

Dear Lord,
Most days, I don't want to face the healing, but I know to make it through this pain I have to face it head on. I can share anything with You because You know emotions better than anyone. I pray You will help me learn to be still yet present and quiet the noise around me. I want to know the sound of Your voice when I hear it and listen more than I speak. Help me engage in healthy coping mechanisms and cling to Your Word.
I pray in Your name, Amen.

The Garden of Growth
• •

Have you noticed if it feels difficult for you to sit in the quiet and the stillness without chaos? If so, in what ways does it feel difficult?

Did God reveal anything during or after your prayer? If so, what?

Day 39
Heart Protection

*And the peace of God, which surpasses all understanding,
will guard your hearts and your minds in Christ Jesus.*
Philippians 4:7

My heart was crushed when I separated from my abuser. It was an intensity of heartbreak I'd never felt before. My heart was crushed because I'd learned the person I was in love with, in reality, had never existed. I was in love with a stranger for close to three years because he wore a mask hiding his true self, and it wasn't until the last few months together his mask began to slip. Was I truly in love? I know my heart was broken into a million pieces, and I wasn't sure how it would be mended or if it was even mendable. I didn't understand the significant pain I felt. I knew I wanted the pain and hurt to stop, and I wanted to go on living the life I was living before my abuser ever came along. I longed for peace in my life again. I also knew once I moved through this situation, I needed God to help me know how to protect my heart against such anguish again. And God came through, as He does, teaching me His ways. As you are looking to heal your broken heart and further protect it from future agony, lean on Jesus and pray this prayer asking Him to give you His unexplainable peace and protection.

*Dear Lord,
I come before You with a heart that is broken and weary and shattered into a million pieces. There are days I actually feel physical pain in my chest. Lord, You understand the depths of*

*my pain and sorrow better than anyone else. I ask for healing
from You for the wounds on my heart and for You to provide
comfort to my soul. Shield my heart from future pain and
disappointment as I want to avoid encountering this same
pain in the future. I pray for a hedge of protection around my
heart and protection from future heartbreak and help make my
broken heart whole and healthy again.
I pray in the mighty name of Jesus, Amen.*

The Garden of Growth

How can you protect your heart while remaining open to love and growth?

Did God reveal anything during or after your prayer? If so, what?

Day 40
Discernment

*Teach me good judgment and knowledge,
for I believe in your commandments.*
Psalm 119:66

While dating my abuser, I frequently made excuses for his actions. When he cancelled plans with me or gave me the silent treatment, I interpreted it as him being tired or having a bad day at work. I often sensed a feeling in my stomach I recurrently disregarded as anxiety, insecurity, and, sometimes, even butterflies of excitement if we were going to be spending time together. I learned I didn't understand how to decipher the feeling I felt in my gut, so I rarely trusted it or paid attention to it. Along with the confusion of my gut feelings, I would feel impending doom. I was constantly waiting for the shoe to drop. I was waiting for the next breakup to happen or the next story he was going to share with me about how he was the victim and someone else was the mean, nasty villain. There was seldom a shortage of these stories from day to day and they would contribute to his deflated moods. His mood set the tone of my mood and it became exhausting and entirely co-dependent.

I now understand my gut feeling was the Holy Spirit attempting to warn me of something–giving me a clue things were not aligning or were not as they seemed and I should get curious and ask questions. Also, the impending doom feeling should not be a typical feeling when in the presence of someone you love. In a healthy relationship, feelings of love, encouragement, trust, and honesty should be present at all times. God can help us understand and equip us with the wisdom and knowledge to decipher our feelings. All we need to do is ask. Pray this prayer asking God to give you wisdom and discernment in your relationships and to help you understand how to decipher your feelings and emotions.

Dear Lord,
I repeatedly have feelings of uneasiness in my stomach. At times, it seems to be butterflies or excitement, while at other times, it could be anxiety or nervousness. I'm unfamiliar and not equipped with godly knowledge and wisdom to properly understand how to decipher these feelings. Lord, I ask You to fill me with the wisdom and discernment I need to work through each feeling in any situation I encounter. I pray You will give me the guidance and help me to handle the learning curve with care.
I pray in Your name, Amen.

The Garden of Growth

What are ways you can work to connect the signals your body is giving you to the feelings you're experiencing?

Did God reveal anything during or after your prayer? If so, what?

Day 41
Pace Your Healing

For everything there is a season, and a time for every matter under heaven...
Ecclesiastes 3:1

When moving through healing from emotional abuse, remember the hurt didn't all happen in a single day. It occurred over time and by someone slowing chipping away for days on end over a long period. Therefore, it is necessary to pace yourself. Even though it is heavy mental and emotional work to heal, you must dive into times of joy and not get overly caught up in recovering from the trauma and working to become a better version of yourself. To avoid becoming fatigued with healing, let loose and do something fun!

I noticed this during my own journey and how exhausted I was some days. When I brought this up to my counselor, she reminded me how difficult the work is mentally and emotionally and to separate myself from it sometimes. I needed to give myself a break and step away from it all and go for a walk and listen to an audiobook aside from a self-help book or listen to a fun podcast aside from the topic of healing trauma or understanding how someone's brain worked. Allow yourself mental and emotional breaks. You don't incessantly have to focus on the betterment of yourself. Ecclesiastes is a good reminder there is a time for everything under heaven. The healing will come. Pray this prayer in the moments you feel fatigued from the work it takes to heal.

Dear Lord,
I understand healing is a journey but help me to understand I don't have to focus on it 100 percent of the time or be so focused on getting through it quickly to move onto the next thing You have for me. Help me to understand the journey can include times of stepping away from deep work and investing in spending time with my friends or family, taking a walk and looking at Your creation, or reading a book involving a silly plot, taking me on an escape to a far away, imaginary land. Remind me to take comfort knowing all things take time and for everything there is a season, including my own healing and rest.
I pray in Your name, Amen.

The Garden of Growth

 List a few ways you can give yourself a break from self-work and self-reflection.

 Did God reveal anything during or after your prayer? If so, what?

Day 42
Free Yourself

Be kind to one another, tenderhearted, forgiving one another, as God in Christ forgave you.
Ephesians 4:32

Forgiving someone who has inflicted pain or caused trauma in our lives is a difficult action to take. As a Christian, I thought forgiving someone required forgetting what they did to me, but I learned the real distinction. We can forgive someone, but it doesn't mean we completely set aside what has happened to us and move forward saying nothing ever happened. However, it does give us permission and allow us to move forward in freedom from being held captive by the unforgettable trauma.

Through the years, I've heard various people say not forgiving your abuser is the same as drinking poison and expecting it to negatively affect the abuser. Unforgiveness holds us captive and in bondage with an angry heart and mind, and the person who caused us pain is not being affected in the least. When we forgive someone, it absolutely does not excuse what they did or the pain they caused, but it allows us to be set free and to move forward freely in our lives and know we have forgiven as God has forgiven us.

It takes time to work up the courage and strength to forgive someone for the pain they caused. It is all part of healing and grieving. I continuously prayed God would soften my heart, humble me, and take the anger away before I could forgive my abuser. This wasn't something I woke up on a random day and said, "I think today is the day I want to forgive." For me to forgive him, it took me spending time talking with God, praying, being in the Word, and lots and lots of tears. Pray this prayer as you are working to move forward and forgive someone who caused you pain, grief, deep sorrow, and heartbreak.

Dear Lord,
I know You have forgiven me time and time again and I am thankful to know I am washed white as snow. I understand You instruct me to forgive others as You have forgiven me, but I'm finding this so hard to do. The pain I've experienced, the heartbreak I'm feeling, the grief and deep sorrow are sometimes more than I can bear, and I become full of anger. When I feel these ways, I can't imagine forgiving someone who has caused me this level of pain. I pray You help me to see forgiving my abuser is going to free me and release me from being held captive because by not forgiving, I'm only causing more pain and damage to myself. Help my heart to soften.
I pray in Your holy, precious name, Amen.

The Garden of Growth

When you think of forgiving someone, what does the process look like to you?

Did God reveal anything during or after your prayer? If so, what?

Day 43
Conquering Fear

... for God gave us a spirit not of fear but of power and love and self-control.
2 Timothy 1:7

Bouts of fear are likely to surface after leaving an abusive relationship because there is lots to heal from. Some legitimate examples are fear of (1) running into the abuser in public and not being prepared mentally or emotionally, (2) the abuser spreading lies and people believing the lies, or (3) the abuser beginning to stalk you, causing you to become a homebody and not live life to the fullest. When I left, I acknowledged those were some of my fears and they required conquering.

Months after my relationship ended, I didn't want to go near the side of town where he lived because I wasn't prepared for how I would react if I saw him. When I'd get together with friends, we'd avoid that side of town and likely end up at my house. I felt at peace in my home, and it became my sanctuary.

Conquering fears is a deeply personal journey, but it is not impossible to do. God's Word reminds us He does not give us a spirit of fear but of power, love, and self-control! When I read that Scripture, I feel empowered by God's Word! How do you feel? God gives us His Word as a guide and a resource for life and a whole book on how we can live peacefully with others and within ourselves. It's all right at our fingertips if we are willing to dig in and go on the journey to find peace and conquer our fears by dissecting them and understanding them at the root. Pray this prayer when you feel fear coming over you or when you are working towards conquering your fears.

Dear Lord,
Thank You for giving me a spirit of power, love, and self-control and not a spirit of fear. Even though I know this to be true, fear still creeps in, and I forget You have given me the power to rebuke the fear in Your holy name. I pray, as I continue to heal from the trauma I experienced, You would remind me in tangible ways I need not fear because You are with me everywhere I go and You will help me to dismantle my fears and understand where they take root. I confess my fears to You today and ask for Your help me in overcoming them.
I pray in Your name, Amen.

Garden of Growth
• •

 How do you face your fears? Would you say it's healthy or unhealthy and why? If they are unhealthy, how can you face your fears in healthy ways?

 Did God reveal anything during or after your prayer? If so, what?

Day 44
Not to Worry

"Therefore do not be anxious about tomorrow, for tomorrow will be anxious for itself. Sufficient for the day is its own trouble."
Matthew 6:34

As someone who suffers from generalized anxiety disorder, this Scripture quickly became a favorite of mine! It is easy to feel bogged down with everyday life on its own, but when adding an abusive relationship to the mix, it doubles the trouble.

I was constantly waiting for the next breakup or the next disaster to arise. I persistently worried about the next hour, the next day, the next phone call, the next, the next, the next. Once my relationship was over, I was then worried about unexpectedly running into him, him spreading lies about me and trying to destroy my character, or even how I would get through the next day.

When we're full of anxiety and worry, Satan loves to have control over us. He laughs and celebrates when we are overtaken by the misery these emotions cause. It is vital to find consolation in God's promises to provide for our every need. We don't have to spend time worrying or being anxious about how we will be taken care of–it's all in God's hands. As the Scripture says, we have enough to worry about for one day, so don't worry about the days and weeks ahead–God's already taking care of it. Pray this prayer when you're feeling worried or anxious. We must lean on Him in times of worry and trust what He says He will do. He is a God of His Word.

Dear Lord,
I call on Your name in my time of worry and anxiousness right now. I bring my concerns to You, knowing You are the God who cares deeply for me. I feel a heaviness and impending doom I can't escape in my own power. Lord, I surrender these burdens to You now. Please take control of my anxious heart and calm my troubled mind. I ask for You to go ahead of me to guide me through this tunnel of doom and gloom and help me see the light on the other side. I ask You to be my rock and foundation, place my feet on solid ground, and pull me up and out from the miry clay.
In Your heavenly name I pray, Amen.

The Garden of Growth

How can you actively combat worry in your daily life?

Did God reveal anything during or after your prayer? If so, what?

Day 45
Source of Energy

I can do all things through him who strengthens me.
Philippians 4:13

Depression crashed down on me like a ton of bricks after my relationship came to an end. I was in excruciating pain from severe autoimmune inflammation, and I struggled to get out of bed, keep up with daily house chores, walk my dogs, or even take a shower. I despised having to take a shower. It was among the hardest undertakings for me because it was a multi-step event, outrageously cumbersome to complete, and I got tired just thinking about it. When I hygienically took care of myself, my body came out feeling clean and refreshed but physically exhausted. It was frustrating knowing I needed to do this task for my physical and mental health, but all I looked forward to was sleeping because if I was awake, I was ruminating.

God provides us with the strength for all things. Not only physically hard things, but all things including the mentally and spiritually difficult situations presented to us. There were numerous times I found myself asking God to pull me out of bed for the day and to please help me by putting my feet on the ground, putting one foot in front of the other to make it to the kitchen, getting the coffee cup from the cabinet, and more. Everything I executed took energy from me, energy I didn't have. However, when I asked God to help me and strengthen me to do these things, day by day, it became easier. It was by no means something I would call "easy," but I made it through by the grace of God and in His strength.

Pray this prayer when you feel you can't go on and when life feels too heavy and full of challenges you know you can't conquer on your own. Ask Him to be your sole source of energy to make it through life's difficulties. There is nothing we can't do with God by our side.

Dear Lord,
Although the typical, everyday responsibilities should be easy to manage, I am not doing well to manage them on my own. Lord, I need You every day and every hour. Please be my source of strength when the nights feel long and when the days feel heavy. I can't neglect my responsibilities and I need to continue forward with life, focusing on my goals and what You have planned for my life. I pray You give me the strength each morning to get through all the tasks needing to be done for the day. I want to successfully keep up with my responsibilities and be honorable and pleasing to You, Lord.
I pray in Your name, Amen.

The Garden of Growth

 Talking to God through prayer helps, but in addition, what practical steps can you take to break down the stigma and promote open dialogue surrounding depression?

 Did God reveal anything during or after your prayer? If so, what?

Day 46
The Solid Rock

The name of the Lord is a strong tower;
the righteous man runs into it and is safe.
Proverbs 18:10

I think of God as a boulder, as a solid rock, and I strive for my life to be built on this foundation. An example of something being built on a solid foundation comes from a story I read during my childhood called *The Three Little Pigs*. This is a story of three pigs and all the different materials they used to build the foundations of their homes. One used straw, another used sticks, and the other used bricks–a solid rock. Their enemy, the Big Bad Wolf, blew down all the houses except the one built with a brick foundation.

There were times I should have run into the arms of my heavenly Father for comfort and safety and instead I ran straight into the arms of my abuser, believing he cared for me and would provide support and comfort. When I think back on these times, it breaks my heart, and I know it broke God's heart in each moment. However, I give myself grace and don't punish myself for what I did because I know how loved and forgiven I am. I desire my life to be solidly built on Christ. We are safe and wrapped in His warmth, power, and vastness and will not be disheveled by anything the enemy, Satan, throws our way. Pray this prayer and return to it as many times as you need to be comforted by Christ. He will give you all the love, stability, and safety you need as He is our strong tower.

Dear Lord,
Thank You for the reminder of Your name being a strong tower and that I can run straight into Your arms for safety. I can have You as a safe haven for my soul and share my deepest thoughts and emotions with You. As Your child, I understand You want me to build my life on You as a firm foundation and to have a strong reliance on You. I pray for guidance in building a stronger and deeply rooted relationship with You as I continue to work through these ninety days of healing. I pray You will continue to reveal truths to me throughout this journey and I will trust You all along the way.
I pray in Your name, Amen.

The Garden of Growth

 What practices or rituals can you incorporate into your daily routine to remind yourself of God's faithfulness as your firm foundation?

 Did God reveal anything during or after your prayer? If so, what?

Day 47
Strength through Weakness

But he said to me, "My grace is sufficient for you, for my power is made perfect in weakness." Therefore I will boast all the more gladly of my weaknesses, so that the power of Christ may rest upon me.
2 Corinthians 12:9

On your journey of healing from abuse, have you been told to "pick yourself up and move on already" or to "just get over it"? I was told those things when it all went up in flames. It made me feel weak, minimized, and whiney. I felt someone else would be able to easily move on from this, but something must be wrong with me since I couldn't push myself and get over it as people were suggesting. This was painful for me. These comments were extremely invalidating to my physical, mental, and emotional pain. I felt more alone than ever before.

I was amazed to learn God's grace is sufficient for me in my weakness. Yes, maybe I did feel weak and maybe I was, but God and His healing power is enough for me. Not only is His grace sufficient, but it is made *perfect* in my weakness. Isn't that freeing and validating?

People who haven't been through a similar experience don't have the context to understand and relate to what we've been through. Keep in mind, people are going to let us down and disappoint us more than we care to admit, but God will never let us down. We can share our story and there are people who will choose to view it as us being weak, but in our weakness, we are made stronger by the power of Christ. Pray this prayer to admit you are weak and ask God to bestow His mighty power upon you.

Dear Lord,
Since all of this happened and I've shared my story, some people tell me I am weak for not being able to quickly get over it. I feel hurt, invalidated, and even full of shame. I want to be a strong person who is resilient and can overcome adversity, but I know I am not equipped to do it alone and not within my own strength. I ask right now for Your perfect power, in my weakness, to be bestowed upon me. I pray You will give me the strength to overcome life's struggles with less difficulty and not be rattled by what other people say or think about me. I believe who You say I am.
I pray in Your name, Amen.

The Garden of Growth

How does the recognition of your weaknesses lead you to rely more fully on God's strength and grace?

Did God reveal anything during or after your prayer? If so, what?

Day 48
Slow to Anger

*Know this, my beloved brothers: let every person be quick
to hear, slow to speak, slow to anger; for the anger of
man does not produce the righteousness of God.*
James 1:19-20

Anger is part of grieving and to completely grieve leaving my abuser, I needed to move through the anger stage more than once. Anger was a difficult emotion for me because I wasn't sure who or what I was angry at or the exact reason I was angry. I yearned to sort out the root of my anger and explore where it came from. I wasn't sure if I was angry at myself for not seeing the red flags earlier, the empty promises made, my abuser in general, or God. And the truth is, I was angry about it all.

I knew there was work for me to do to return to a healthy heart condition, continue healing overall, and work through the stages of grief. I didn't want to remain in a state of anger or hold a grudge. I longed to be set free from the bondage of anger and to see what plans God held in His hands for my life. I desired to be open to what trustworthy Christian mentors wanted to speak into my life and learn from other survivors of abuse.

Praying and asking God for open ears and a quiet mouth, as I've always been a talker, was quite a challenge. I needed to learn to listen more than I spoke, but on the other hand, I also wanted to share my story, have my feelings validated, and try to talk things out to make sense of the mess. Pray this prayer when you feel anger rising or when you're stuck in the anger stage of healing. Ask God to quiet your mind and mouth and open your ears to know God's voice and to be open to hear what trusted mentors say when speaking truth into your life.

Dear Lord,
I am full of anger, and even though I understand this to be part of the stages of grief and healing, I don't want to be held in bondage by the stronghold I know anger can cause in my life. As Your Word says, I want to be quick to listen, especially to You, slow to speak, and slow to anger. I want to experience Your righteousness, and I understand I am unable to do this with anger in my heart. Guide me to those who will speak truth into my life and open my ears to listen to what they have to say. Let me not be argumentative or overly defensive, but open to their words.
I pray in Your name, Amen.

The Garden of Growth
• •

How can you recognize and address the root causes of your anger and seek healing and restoration in those areas?

Did God reveal anything during or after your prayer? If so, what?

Day 49
Mind Renewal

Do not be conformed to this world, but be transformed by the renewal of your mind, that by testing you may discern what is the will of God, what is good and acceptable and perfect.
Romans 12:2

My mind felt different when I withdrew from my abusive relationship. It wasn't immediate, but after some time of immersing myself into my healing journey, I felt the fog starting to lift and the distorted reality starting to be revealed. I was finally beginning to see more clearly. I was beginning to see the truth. The longer I worked on healing, praying, and moving forward with tools I learned in therapy, the more I felt the shift happening in the way I was thinking and the way I viewed life and other people. The best way to describe it is the swirling chaos slowed down in my brain and my nervous system learned to calm down and live a less emotionally demanding life of its own!

Glory to God! I believe the shift was Him renewing my mind and reminding me the commotion I previously felt was not His will for my life and He declared better plans for me on the horizon. I prayed God would clear the haze from my mind, enabling me to understand the traumatizing events more clearly and to discern truth and reality before entering any future situation—whether romantic, friendly, or professional. Pray this prayer today and return to it when you feel foggy-minded and need reality to be more visible. God will provide hope for your future through a renewed mind and new eyes.

Faithful Lord,
Thank You for Your goodness. I come seeking a renewed mind with clarity for my thoughts and a new reality. I pray You help the fog to lift and for me to clearly see and understand what happened to me at the hand of my abuser. Help me to release the lies from my mind instilled in me during the relationship and to replace those lies with truths and promises from Your Word. Guide me by faith and grant me the courage to move onward toward a transformed mind full of joy, positivity, and wisdom.
I pray in Your name, Amen.

The Garden of Growth

How can you surrender your own future desires to God's will?

Did God reveal anything during or after your prayer? If so, what?

Day 50
Nothing Can Separate

*Neither height nor depth, nor anything else in all creation,
will be able to separate us from the love of God in Christ
Jesus our Lord.*
Romans 8:39

Throughout my relationship, there were certain times I felt distant from God. It turns out I felt this way because I unknowingly put my abuser on a pedestal. It inadvertently happened when he inflicted fear, manipulation, and emotional dependency, and it clouded my judgement, leaving me to compromise for the sake of appeasing him. I wish he hadn't come above God. Regardless of how hard I tried to revive my relationship with the Lord while actively in relationship with my abuser, I couldn't get myself there. I know from reading God's Word He was always with me and He waited with open arms for me to return to Him.

I am grateful God didn't hold it against me when I wasn't connecting and relying on Him and I wasn't living an authentic, godly life. I *wanted* to be a messenger for Him, but I tried to pacify my abuser first to earn the love, time, and attention I desperately craved. I praise God for not give up on me, tossing me to the wayside, and eternally shunning me. Even after all I did to feel I didn't deserve God's grace and love, He pursued me, ran after me, and called out for me to return. Pray today's prayer with an attitude of gratitude to God for His act of pursuing His children despite our choices. Also, ask Him for humble reminders of His presence and signs indicating how nothing will separate you from His unfailing love.

Dear Lord,
I graciously thank You for Your everlasting love and Your constant pursuit of me. When I thought You would want nothing to do with me, You showed me what true love is. You embraced me, expressed Your fervent love for me, and desired for me to run unabashedly to You and to never let go. Thank You, oh, Lord. Please keep me open to Your presence and Your will for my life. In times I feel distant or separated from You, I pray You eternally remind me nothing can separate us.
I pray in Your name, Amen.

The Garden of Growth

 When you imagine God pursuing you, running after you, and waiting with open arms for you to return to Him, what emotions do you feel? Describe the scene you envision in your mind when you imagine this. Is anything happening around you? Are other people around? How's the weather? Are there any specific scents you notice?

 Did God reveal anything during or after your prayer? If so, what?

Day 51
God as the Guide

If any of you lacks wisdom, let him ask God, who gives generously to all without reproach, and it will be given him.
James 1:5

After leaving my abuser, it became clear I'd lacked wisdom during my relationship. I'd lacked the knowledge and understanding of what I was going through at the time I was experiencing it. I've since learned the value of wisdom. It encompasses patience, discernment, integrity, and compassion. As a teenager and young adult, I recall times when people would attempt to share advice with me and I would say, "It was different when you were growing up. You just don't understand." However, wisdom can be shared by someone with a similar experience (though no one's story is exactly the same), through reflection and prayer and during moments of solitude.

There isn't a time when we have all the wisdom we'll ever need. Being filled with wisdom is a lifelong journey and a constant opportunity for growth and understanding. Obtaining wisdom takes humility and the willingness to listen to wise counsel in whatever way God reveals. Since I have been healing, I have learned an immense amount about the journey of others. I have gained an understanding about what tools work for me if I feel myself starting to slip back into unhealthy habits. If I didn't have humility, I would miss out on the wisdom opportunities God has for me. Say this prayer asking

God for a mindset embodying the qualities to hold wisdom and for Him to reveal wisdom, and opportunities for you to gain wisdom, in a way you can easily understand.

Dear Lord,
Wisdom is a gift You freely and generously give if I ask. So, Lord, today I am humbly asking for You to fill me with wisdom. I know wisdom can come in different forms, so I pray You will guide me to the right people to speak into my life and allow me to be quick to listen to what You want to reveal to me in times of solitude. In moments of uncertainty, help me to focus on You as my source of wisdom and trust in Your guidance to lead in all areas of my life.
I pray in Your name, Amen.

The Garden of Growth

How does a posture of openness to God's wisdom impact your relationships, decision-making processes, and overall sense of peace and fulfillment?

Did God reveal anything during or after your prayer? If so, what?

Day 52
Spending Time Alone

And after he had dismissed the crowds, he went up on the mountain by himself to pray. When evening came, he was there alone.
Matthew 14:23

This Scripture began to stand out to me within the last few years. It comes after Jesus fed the crowd of 5,000 with only two fish and five loaves of bread. Jesus maintained a busy day of performing miracles and teaching crowds, so he retreated to the mountaintop to be in solitude and pray. I see this as an example of how I should live my life. Since I am often busy with my full-time job, my dog treat business, taking care of my fur babies, trying to keep up with household chores, and lately, writing this book, I easily forget to slow down, reflect, and rest.

Slowing down, resting, and reflecting were important steps for my healing. It wasn't solely important for my mental health, but it was necessary for my nervous system to understand the state of calmness and not live in fight-or-flight mode 24/7. Spending time alone allowed me to learn and utilize self-soothing practices, such as journaling, praying, being in nature, and spending time in God's Word. God wants us to find time to rest, reset, and spiritually renew ourselves. Say this prayer when life feels full of distractions, stress, or chaos. God hears our prayers and if you allow Him, He will help calm your soul.

Dear Lord,
My life feels stressful, full of distraction, and at times, chaotic.
I know spending time alone and setting aside intentional time
to calm my racing thoughts is good for my soul. Sometimes I
want my life busy enough to avoid facing any of the hard stuff
I know I need to deal with. Lord, I pray You will help me to feel
satisfied spending time alone. Fill me with reminders that the time
I'm spending alone is helpful to my healing journey, but more
importantly, is deepening my relationship with You.
I pray in Your name, Amen.

The Garden of Growth

 What practices or activities bring you the most rest and rejuvenation during times of solitude, and how can you incorporate them into your regular routine?

 Did God reveal anything during or after your prayer? If so, what?

Day 53
Set Strong Boundaries

*Do not enter the path of the wicked,
and do not walk in the way of the evil.
Avoid it; do not go on it;
turn away from it and pass on.*
Proverbs 4:14-15

Throughout my life, I thought I held strong boundaries when it came to relationships, but instead I discovered I held standards. I learned through therapy and support groups, boundaries are what someone uses to maintain self-worth and keep from entering toxic interactions, but standards are qualities proving evident before becoming involved with someone whether platonically, professionally, or romantically. If I'd known how to set strong boundaries, I believe a lot of the pain and hurt I endured could have been avoided. I also believe I would have been able to turn away from my relationship and move forward onto a healthier path much sooner.

Proverbs 4:14-15 instructs us not to *intentionally* walk down the path of wicked with evildoers and not to engage in behaviors or activities compromising our morals or leading to wrongdoing. A key point to draw out from this passage is the part on intentionality. The repetitive nature of the Scripture saying, "avoid it," "do not go on it," and "turn away from it" explains there is a difference between *choosing* to go down a path of the wicked with a wrongdoer and being *manipulated* to do so. In the case of abuse, this path is not chosen intentionally by the survivor. The survivor is often preyed upon, targeted, and magnetized into interaction. Pray this prayer asking God to protect you and help you avoid becoming prey to any future abuse.

Dear Lord,
Even though I was preyed upon, I suffered a significant amount of pain and trauma due to my lack of boundaries. I have forgiven myself and have also given myself grace because I didn't fully understand the extent of what boundaries were before I began healing. I now know I need strong boundaries going forward to avoid walking down the path of wickedness and engaging with evildoers, even if unintentionally. I also pray You will help others to realize the boundaries I put in place in my own life are a way to protect me and not a fence I've put up to keep everyone at a distance. I ask for You to help me uphold my standards of a healthy relationship and be able to set healthy boundaries moving forward.
I pray in Your name, Amen.

The Garden of Growth

Write a list of boundaries you have in place for your relationships. Discuss them with a counselor, support group, or trusted friend/mentor.

Did God reveal anything during or after your prayer? If so, what?

Day 54
Rooted in Resilience

Not only that, but we rejoice in our sufferings, knowing that suffering produces endurance, and endurance produces character, and character produces hope, and hope does not put us to shame, because God's love has been poured into our hearts through the Holy Spirit who has been given to us.
Romans 5:3-5

While my breakup was still fresh, a friend inquired, "Do you think down the road you will look back and realize how much you learned from this?" Right then, I was incredibly hurt and frustrated by her question, I responded with, "No! This is the most painful and confusing thing I've ever experienced. I can't imagine I'll be able to look back and see any good come from this." Now, if you knew this friend, you would know she is a positive person who tries to find good in most situations, so she asked this strictly to encourage me and help me realize it wasn't going to be painful forever. She'd known me for many years, and this was the most broken down she'd ever seen me, and she later expressed to me how concerned she was for me.

I would never wish abuse in any way, shape, or form on anyone, but because of what I bore, how I persevered and the resiliency I developed, I am more compassionate, hopeful, creative, joyful, and peaceful. I suffered, but through my suffering, I gained character, transformation, and bundles of hope. I've drawn strength from faith, my relationship with God, and authentic connection with others. So, to my friend who asked me the question, yes, I have been able to look back and see all I've learned through the suffering. It doesn't make it any easier to accept what happened to me or the pain and trauma it caused, but through the very thing that caused me so much pain, I am fulfilling my calling and my purpose of encouraging and pouring into others and honoring God by giving Him the glory for what He brought me through. As you heal, I pray you will see your suffering through a lens of hope and resiliency. Pray this prayer asking God to give you a perspective to see your strength and the love He pours into your heart.

Dear Lord,
I never wanted to endure the abuse and trauma I encountered,
but I was not aware of the strength and perseverance I
encompassed. I know You didn't cause this to happen, but You
were with me through it all and prepared to rescue me. Pain
and suffering are part of the human experience and You suffered
worse than anyone ever has; You understand pain at the deepest
levels. Lord, I want to see growth in myself. I pray You will
give me courage, perseverance, and hope as I navigate my way
through this time of difficulty and adversity.
I pray in Your name, Amen.

The Garden of Growth

How can you use your experiences of overcoming adversity to inspire and encourage others?

Did God reveal anything during or after your prayer? If so, what?

Day 55
No More Bondage

*O Lord my God, I cried to you for help,
and you have healed me.*
Psalm 30:2

There are many names for God, but two of my favorites are Deliverer (Psalm 34:17-19) and Healer (Exodus 15:26). When I cry out to God, I know without a doubt He hears me and cares about what I'm going through. I knew part of healing required me to break ties with my abuser and the labels I attached to myself; however, I knew I couldn't do this in my own power. I passionately desired to break the bond and be mentally free from the hold on me. I needed God to do what He does best and break the chains I felt were attached to me and dragging behind me with every step I took. Figuratively speaking, these chains were heavy and they represented the demoralizing labels I'd adopted as my identity.

I would play worship music in my house and ask God to loosen and remove the chains. I didn't want to believe the lies of the enemy and the labels placed on me of *broken*, *unworthy*, and *unlovable*. Unfortunately, I found it hard to escape them because of the shell of a person I'd become. This took time of praying and continually humbling myself, asking God to do this for me. I knew once I prayed to God and asked for release from this, He'd already healed me and removed those labels from me because they were *not* how He described me. It was *not* the name or the identity He gave me. It was *me* who needed to believe God removed the labels and *I* needed to remove the labels from myself. God did His part, now it was necessary for me to do mine by trusting who God says I am and not who the enemy said I was. I was holding myself in bondage after God had already released me! He will release you from the bondage you feel. Pray this prayer asking Him to set you free mentally, emotionally, physically, spiritually, and/or financially from your abuser. Cry out to Him and He will take care of you! Once you have done this, believe it has been done so you can move forward in freedom!

Dear Lord,
I come before You with a heavy but hopeful heart, seeking Your grace and strength in the midst of my struggles. You know the pain and suffering I have endured at the hands of my abuser, and You see how the wounds left scars on my mind, heart, body, and spirit. Lord, I am crying out for release from this oppression and for freedom in every aspect of my life. Let Your truth and light shine through the darkness. I surrender myself completely into Your hands, trusting in Your power to set me free. May Your grace sustain me through every hardship.
I pray in Your name, Amen.

The Garden of Growth

What labels are you still holding on to that are keeping you from experiencing true freedom from your abuser?

Did God reveal anything during or after your prayer? If so, what?

Day 56
My Hiding Place

*You are a hiding place for me;
you preserve me from trouble;
you surround me with shouts of deliverance.*
Psalm 32:7

In times of trouble, it is a relief to know God is our hiding place, full of rest, peace, and protection. Many times, I begged to crawl into a hole, disappear, and hide away from the world. I didn't want to face reality, and I really wanted to completely forget what I'd endured. However, I couldn't literally crawl into a hole and disappear because I'm an adult and I have responsibilities and bills to pay. Since literally hiding wasn't an option, I'm grateful I could do this metaphorically by allowing God to protect me under the shadow of His wings.

Eventually, facing reality is unavoidable when healing from trauma or abuse, but I found God to be my security and protection while I healed. Not only did He merely protect me, but He delivered me from an evil situation and He was my defender. I drew near to God and He heard my heartfelt prayers and drew near to me. He gave me confidence and assurance to move forward each day under His protection and in His presence by providing me with a hedge of peace and a shield from harm and fear. I am evidence of God's restorative power. He restores the broken and delivers us from evil, and I believe when we seek Him, He listens and provides. Pray this prayer for God to be your hiding place and your protector and deliverer from evil. Trust in His unfailing love and find refuge from life's storms.

Dear Lord,
Sometimes I need a hiding place from the world, and I want to find my hiding place under the shadow of Your wings. Lord, I pray earnestly for You to be my hiding place when I'm seeking refuge, my protector and deliverer from evil, and for Your hedge of peace and shield from trouble. I don't want to hide using worldly coping mechanisms, but instead, I want to remain in relationship with You and stand strong on Your Word and promises. Thank You for Your unfailing and unwavering love.
I pray in Your name, Amen.

The Garden of Growth

When are the times you recall God protecting you and hiding you under the shadow of His wings, sheltering you from harm?

Did God reveal anything during or after your prayer? If so, what?

Day 57
Healthy Love

Love is patient and kind; love does not envy or boast; it is not arrogant or rude. It does not insist on its own way; it is not irritable or resentful; it does not rejoice at wrongdoing, but rejoices with the truth. Love bears all things, believes all things, hopes all things, endures all things.
1 Corinthians 13:4-7

Paul described the qualities and power of love in 1 Corinthians 13. While this is a common Scripture read at weddings, it can also be applied to bring healing and wholeness to our lives as individuals. We can keep this Scripture at the forefront of our minds, especially if we're planning on having healthy connections in the future. Something I found constantly confusing during my relationship was the love being one-sided. I was holding on for any glimmer of hope or sign showing he loved me, but just didn't know how to properly express it. What was even more confusing was he'd portrayed these qualities in the beginning of our relationship, and once I was in too deep, I kept thinking the man from the beginning would show himself again. I would receive tiny glimpses of who I met in the beginning, but he never stayed around long.

A bit of practical information I've learned about healthy love throughout my healing is it must be reciprocated from both sides; it is not one-sided, effortless, or easy. Love takes work from both sides and it's not always a

50/50 split. Some days the effort is 80/20 and others it's 60/40. Love is about teamwork and grace, trust and respect, and patience and kindness. I believe this kind of romantic love does exist for survivors of abuse. Believe this exists for you and pray this prayer, asking God to reveal genuine, healthy, romantic love when it comes around if it's His will for your life.

Dear Lord,
Thank You for the depiction of healthy love laid out in Your Word with the understanding it brings healing and wholeness to my life. Love is such a gift You have given. Lord, let my love be a source of blessing, joy, and transformation, enhancing the lives of those around me and bringing glory to Your name. Since I have been involved in relationships comprised of unhealthy love, I pray You will make it clear to me when there is a healthy romantic love for me to embrace; one that is genuine and honoring to You.
I pray in Your name, Amen.

The Garden of Growth

How would you benefit from experiencing the love described in 1 Corinthians 13:4-7, and in what tangible ways would you want someone to demonstrate this kind of love?

Did God reveal anything during or after your prayer? If so, what?

Day 58
God Restores

I will restore to you the years
that the swarming locust has eaten,
the hopper, the destroyer, and the cutter,
my great army, which I sent among you.
Joel 2:25

My grandma sent me a card with Joel 2:25 on the front shortly after the breakup. She didn't know the reason my relationship had ended or the extent of what I'd endured. She didn't know I did in fact feel as though I'd lost years of my life to someone. I put the card on my refrigerator, and I returned countless times to the kitchen to read those words to remind myself of God's restoring power and how I would one day be made whole again. That card meant so much to me. I have since moved and I still have it hanging on my fridge.

This Scripture remained in the back of my mind, reminding me of God's promises of restoration, renewal, healing, and transformation. It reminded me, aside from my suffering and hardship, there was a season of abundance and blessing ahead. Hallelujah! I believed God would pull me out of the pit and pour out His grace, faithfulness, and mercy. I could feel God was going to do something great in my life to bring glory to His name. God's plan for our lives is and forever will be bigger than we could ever imagine for ourselves. I will continue to trust Him and His restorative power in my life and I hope you will too! Pray this prayer, asking God to restore everything lost at the hands of your abuser. Ask God to transform your life in ways you could never do or imagine for yourself. God is trustworthy, loving, and good and will change your life for the better.

Dear Lord,
Thank You for Your promise of making all things new. I trust in Your redeeming power. You will redeem my past and restore everything lost or stolen in every area of my life. My heart is open to Your healing touch and transformative power in my life. Change my life in the greatest of ways to bring glory to Your name and exemplify Your grace and power.
I pray in Your heavenly name, Amen.

The Garden of Growth

How can you trust God more fully as you wait for His restoration and renewal in your life?

Did God reveal anything during or after your prayer? If so, what?

Day 59
Shoulder to Shoulder

Bear one another's burdens, and so fulfill the law of Christ.
Galatians 6:2

Finding support after leaving an abuser can be challenging. The abuser probably appeared to be a genuine, caring, and trustworthy person to those on the outside looking in, which is not unusual. I'm thankful a few close friends and my mom were willing to listen and pray earnestly for me to heal. I am thankful for the community of people who walked beside me and showed compassion for me.

It is essential to seek community and support and provide the same to others in return. God commands us to actively participate in the lives of other believers and share in both joy and sorrow (Romans 12:15, Galatians 6:2). Having others come alongside me during my time of healing helped to lighten the load. It helped knowing others were walking in solidarity with me. Having a support system provided encouragement and comfort by carrying out acts of service and committing to prayer. All this helped make my healing and grieving more feasible and bearable.

I distinctly recall a time my mom came over when I was deep in the pit of depression and my dishes and laundry were piled high and many other chores remained undone. I was embarrassed at the state of my house, but she came over without hesitation and without judgement and told me to rest on the couch while she took care of those tasks for me. Having her handle those chores for me lifted weight from my shoulders I didn't realize I was carrying. Another time, I was on the phone with a friend, and she said she heard the pain in my voice and the next thing I knew, she was at my front door, stopping by to hug me and check on me face-to-face. I'm thankful beyond measure for my support system that showed up and walked alongside me. Say this prayer asking God to provide you with a support system comprised of people who show up and walk alongside you in your grief and throughout your healing journey.

Dear Lord,
Thank You for designing us to live in community with one another, to carry each other's burdens, and to celebrate our joys together. I pray You will provide me with caring and understanding people who can offer wisdom, compassion, and support throughout my journey. The enemy wants to keep me without support in my life, causing me to feel alone and isolated, but I pray the right people will come into my life, lifting me up with encouragement and connection pleasing to You.
I pray in Your name, Amen.

The Garden of Growth

What qualities do you value most in a supportive relationship or community, and how can you actively seek out or nurture those connections?

Did God reveal anything during or after your prayer? If so, what?

Day 60
The Serenity Prayer

Submit yourselves therefore to God. Resist the devil, and he will flee from you.
James 4:7

I attended a program through a local church called Celebrate Recovery (CR) to work through codependency hang-ups I was facing. CR is a Christ-centered, twelve-step program started at a church in California in 1991.[19] While I participated in the program, I learned the full serenity prayer and realized while this prayer is mainly about surrendering to circumstances outside our control, it is also about surrendering to God's guidance and His will for our lives. James 4:7 and the Serenity Prayer both highlight attitudes of surrender, acceptance, and action, which are foundational to healing and growth.

Throughout my healing journey, I returned to this prayer over and over because it encompassed a great deal of what I considered necessary for a healthy future: (1) accepting what I couldn't change, (2) changing what I could, (3) being present, (4) understanding it was necessary to move through the hardship to hold the peace I desperately longed for, and (5) trusting God would restore and redeem me by surrendering to Him.

I am now sharing this prayer with you! Pray this prayer, write it down on a piece of paper, and keep it in your purse or your pocket or type it into your phone for quick and easy access. Whatever you need to do to have this prayer be accessible and for you to return to it repeatedly throughout your journey, do it.

God, grant me the serenity
to accept the things I cannot change,
the courage to change the things I can,
and the wisdom to know the difference.
Living one day at a time,
enjoying one moment at a time;
accepting hardship as a pathway to peace;
taking, as Jesus did,
this sinful world as it is,
not as I would have it;
trusting that You will make all things right
if I surrender to Your will;
so that I may be reasonably happy in this life
and supremely happy with You forever in the next.
Amen.

I admire the effort you are putting forth! You have completed the thirty days of Truth through Prayer! I'm optimistic your prayer life has improved and you are now able to talk with God more like a friend over a delicious cup of coffee or tea and have special encounters with Him. I hope you have seen prayers answered throughout these last thirty days and you will continue praying, whether referencing prayers from this section or talking with God freely on your own. He loves you, and you have a hotline straight to heaven.

The Garden of Growth

In what ways can you surrender your pain to God, trusting in His ability to bring healing and restoration?

Did God reveal anything during or after your prayer? If so, what?

Section Three
Truth through Rediscovery

Then the nations that are left all around you shall know that I am the LORD; I have rebuilt the ruined places and replanted that which was desolate. I am the LORD; I have spoken, and I will do it.
Ezekiel 36:36

I felt empty, like a shell of who I once was after my relationship ended. I no longer enjoyed things in life that once filled me with unexplainable joy and happiness. I was no longer the creative, happy, bubbly person I once was, and I felt stripped down to the bare bones. It was overwhelmingly disheartening. I started doing activities by myself to try to rediscover what I liked and what brought me joy. Then, after a while on my path of healing, I returned to places my abuser and I visited, but I didn't go alone. I went back with friends or family; people I knew I was safe with and who I knew loved and supported me in my healing journey. This allowed me to make new and positive memories with people I cared about deeply.

Section Three will provide you with thirty days of activities to help you rediscover yourself by learning what you love to do and finding your joy and happiness in the mundane things of life once again. Start slowly as you work through this section, and to keep things simple, do these activities in order. There's no need to rush this part. I'm over three years out of my relationship and I'm still learning things I really enjoy and appreciate in life since doing a significant amount of healing and post-traumatic growth. Take each rediscovery activity in stride. If it takes you longer than thirty days to get through this section, don't be discouraged. You can choose to spend more than one day on an activity, or maybe you find there is something about an activity triggering you and you need more time to work through it. There is no official timeline for how long it takes to fully heal and grieve. Be proud of the work you have done up to this point. You have finished sixty days of understanding and prayer and are now ready to rediscover the joy, passion, beauty, and love God placed inside you. I'm incredibly proud of you for coming this far. Don't give up on yourself. You deserve to live a prosperous and abundant life free from abuse.

Day 61
Deserving Gestures

Bless the Lord, O my soul,
and forget not all his benefits,
who forgives all your iniquity,
who heals all your diseases,
who redeems your life from the pit,
who crowns you with steadfast love and mercy,
who satisfies you with good
so that your youth is renewed like the eagle's.
Psalm 103:2-5

When reading through the Scripture above, it's evident all God has freely done for us. And the best part is, He did it all without us even asking Him! It's who God is.

For today's activity, make a list of the nice gestures you wish the abuser would have done to make you feel special, wanted, and loved throughout the course of the relationship. Here are a few ideas to get the wheels turning: (1) being asked out on a date, (2) going to dinner together, (3) playing a game together, (4) having a movie night, (5) giving you flowers–really anything you wish they'd have done for you. You will use this list as the starting point in tomorrow's rediscovery activity.

God does beautiful things for His children and there is nothing He won't do to rebuild, heal, and redeem. Keep this Scripture close as a reminder of God's faithfulness.

The Garden of Growth

 Reflect on what you felt before, during, and after today's activity.

Day 62
Be Kind

*He fulfills the desire of those who fear him;
he also hears their cry and saves them.*
Psalm 145:19

It's time to pull out the list from yesterday's activity. Read over it carefully, meditating on each item listed, asking yourself why each particular gesture would have helped you to feel loved and cherished. After reflecting, it's time to choose at least one item from the list and do it for yourself! Why not? You're allowed to be kind and do nice gestures for yourself and it's not considered selfish. It's loving and generous, caring and precious. It doesn't have to be a special occasion to take yourself out for a nice dinner or cook something fancy at home. You don't have to have an upcoming vacation planned to get your nails done or to get a foot massage at the spa. You can book your own appointment or do it for yourself at home as a form of self-care. You are allowed to love yourself and treat yourself with kindness and respect. Perhaps this feels hard because of what you've been through, but you are precious and deserve to be deeply loved.

Think of this Scripture as a reminder of God's intention for your life. God has your best interest at heart. He wants your desires to be fulfilled and for you to cry out to Him for His will for your life. He wants you to seek out His guidance forever and always.

The Garden of Growth
• •

   Reflect on what you felt before, during, and after today's activity.

Day 63
Alone isn't Lonely

*For God alone, O my soul, wait in silence,
for my hope is from him.
He only is my rock and my salvation,
my fortress; I shall not be shaken.
On God rests my salvation and my glory;
my mighty rock, my refuge is God.
Trust in him at all times, O people;
pour out your heart before him;
God is a refuge for us.*
Psalm 62:5-8

I hope you're feeling great after doing something for yourself yesterday. Today's activity is focused on spending a specific amount of time unplugged and alone—alone with your feelings, thoughts, fears, joys, challenges, accomplishments, and heartaches. It appears when society sees people alone, they believe them to be lonely. Personally, I have learned to downright enjoy my time alone; I don't feel the slightest bit lonely. Truthfully, I felt lonelier with my abuser than I do being single.

Looking at the Scripture, silence and rest is refuge for your soul. For today, determine the amount of time you want to devote to this activity.

Maybe you only feel ready to spend an hour alone to start, or maybe you are prepared to spend the whole day unplugged and really challenge yourself. Do what feels comfortable today, and you can repeat this activity and increase the duration later down the road.

In preparation, take a deep breath and silence the noise of your surroundings and your mind. Let your soul and mind rest in the silent shelter of the Lord today. Talk to Him in your alone time and let Him know what's hurting you, ticking you off, bringing you joy, triggering pain, and anything else on your heart or mind. Then, wait in silence to hear what He wants to pour into your life today. Prepare to encounter God and hear His voice.

The Garden of Growth

Reflect on what you felt before, during, and after today's activity.

Day 64
Peace in the Park

By awesome deeds you answer us with righteousness,
O God of our salvation,
the hope of all the ends of the earth
and of the farthest seas;
the one who by his strength established the mountains,
being girded with might;
who stills the roaring of the seas,
the roaring of their waves,
the tumult of the peoples,
so that those who dwell at the ends of the earth are in awe
at your signs.
You make the going out of the morning and the evening to
shout for joy.
Psalm 65:5-8

Wow, friend. I wish I could sit down with you and hear about your experience this far. I'm trusting there's been a good start to rediscovering yourself. Today, I thought it would be fun for you to go to a park or somewhere with a bench, out in nature, take your favorite drink or snack (heck, why not both?!?), and enjoy God's creation. Start by looking around, being present, and breathing in the fresh air. Then, think about the details in each masterpiece. For example, look at a tree and imagine all there is to it. It started from a seed, then it grew a strong root system. Next, if it's a big tree, think about how many decades it grew to become the size it is today! Then the tree grew branches and leaves or fruit depending on the kind of tree. It's not just "a tree." God designed a plan for the tree and each thing He placed into this world, including you.

Reflecting on today's Scripture and the time you spent in God's magnificent creation, I hope you found yourself in awe. I hope you find yourself singing for joy with the birds in the mornings and you look in amazement at the sky, understanding wholeheartedly you are part of God's creation.

The Garden of Growth

Reflect on what you felt before, during, and after today's activity.

Day 65
Stability and Strength

Finally, be strong in the Lord and in the strength of his might.
Ephesians 6:10

Each day these activities take time, and some are more challenging than others. Today's activity is all about grounding yourself, being present, and gaining a sense of strength and stability. Go outside—barefoot—and walk towards the grass. Take note of how it feels walking on different surfaces towards the grass. Are they smooth, rough, soft, or hard? Now make your way to the grass and sit down, lay down, or stand in the grass. Whatever you feel most comfortable doing is fine! Now it's time to engage your senses. Feel the grass with your fingers and toes. Does it make you feel itchy? Does the grass feel dry, lacking water? Can you smell it? How would you describe the smell? Does it look recently mowed? Take note of anything you notice with your five senses about the grass and the environment around you.

The technique of grounding is a great tool to help when sorting through difficult emotions and navigating challenging situations or to calm your wandering mind. It's a great way to gain clarity and resiliency. The Lord is your strength, and He created nature and everything in it, so standing on or sitting in the grass is like being embraced in God's mighty strength (or a big hug from the Lord), as the Scripture says!

The Garden of Growth
· ·

Reflect on what you felt before, during, and after today's activity.

Day 66
Treat Yourself

A man who is kind benefits himself,
but a cruel man hurts himself.
Proverbs 11:7

Today is another activity geared towards being kind to yourself. There are a few days throughout the rediscovery section surrounding this topic! The intention is for you to understand that taking care of yourself and filling your cup will help you to better love and serve others. As flight attendants say on an airplane: you must first put on your own mask before helping others put on theirs. For today's activity, think of something you would consider to be a real treat for yourself. Is it a fun, responsible night out on the town with a friend, a deliciously flavorful meal, a ninety-minute massage at a fancy spa with a robe and slippers, or a day of spontaneous adventure with obstacle courses, ropes courses, and zip lines? The possibilities are endless! The point for today is to do something considerably special for yourself, something you wouldn't typically do on any regular day, and savor it.

This way, you can start to dig in a little deeper and begin finding the joys in life again. When you are loving towards yourself and treating yourself to enjoyable activities or services, you are reminding yourself how you should be treated with kindness. You don't need to withhold excitement from your life. You are free to treat yourself to the things you consider luxuries. What are you waiting for? Go do something you enjoy today! I wish I was there to tag along!

The Garden of Growth

Reflect on what you felt before, during, and after today's activity.

Day 67
Setting Goals

Do you not know that in a race all the runners run, but only one receives the prize? So run that you may obtain it. Every athlete exercises self-control in all things. They do it to receive a perishable wreath, but we an imperishable. So I do not run aimlessly; I do not box as one beating the air.
1 Corinthians 9:24-26

Today is all about goal setting. Do you feel an amazing sense of triumph and excitement when you complete something? It could be a chore at home you procrastinated on and you finally put your boots to the ground and finished it. Or maybe it was a task at work lingering on your to-do list and you finally found time in your busy schedule to mark it as complete. Whether it's a personal or professional accomplishment, it consistently gives me a sense of pride, and quite honestly, relief, when I accomplish a goal or a task.

There are various goals you can set for yourself to help rebuild your confidence. Here are a few examples to get your mind in motion: (1) learn to play an instrument, (2) learn a new language, (3) become proficient in a specific software program, (4) run a marathon, (5) pay off a lingering debt, (6) complete a do-it-yourself (DIY) project, or (7) explore a new hobby, such as photography or gardening. To start, I suggest making your first goal something fairly easy to attain because I don't want you to feel discouraged or frustrated if you're having a hard time with it. This is meant to be a fun, encouraging way to explore reestablishing your confidence and to serve as a growth opportunity. After all, the main goal we are after is to spend eternity with Jesus. Now, go set some goals and recognize all God has given you the ability to achieve! I believe in you!

The Garden of Growth

 Reflect on what you felt before, during, and after today's activity.

Day 68
Soulful Reflections

But the Lord said to Samuel, "Do not look on his appearance or on the height of his stature, because I have rejected him. For the Lord sees not as man sees: man looks on the outward appearance, but the Lord looks on the heart."
1 Samuel 16:7

Today for your activity, I encourage you to complete a few soulful reflections. Reflecting inward and having the self-awareness to do it isn't a trait everyone possesses but it's a good trait to have, especially when you are healing from emotional abuse. You can engage in deeper introspection by asking yourself open-ended questions. A few you can start with are: (1) what are my core values and beliefs, (2) what challenges and/or obstacles am I currently facing, (3) what brings me joy and fulfillment, and (4) how do I prioritize my time and energy? Although I thoroughly encourage you to journal your reflections to look back on later and recognize your growth, do what you feel is most comfortable.

Rest assured: God knows our hearts better than we do. If you feel stuck on something and don't know how to answer, ask God to provide you with guidance for answers to the questions you are reflecting on. Be still and listen. As the Scripture says above, God looks on the heart. Look to Him to provide you with insight.

The Garden of Growth
• •

Reflect on what you felt before, during, and after today's activity.

Day 69
Sacred Silence

I rise before dawn and cry for help;
I hope in your words.
My eyes are awake before the watches of the night,
that I may meditate on your promise.
Psalm 119:147-148

For today, find time to set aside for silence and prioritize time with God. I flip-flop back and forth between rising before the sun and being a night owl, and I find my choice aligns with different seasons in my life. When I have significant stress, I notice I rise before the sun because my mind can't stop swirling with all I need to get done in the day ahead. When I have less stress, I can stay up with the owls and sleep in long after the sun has risen. But my favorite is getting up before the sun rises, when everything is calm and quiet as the nightlight's soft rays illuminate my home. It's the most tranquil part of my day and when I feel closest to Jesus. It's before the demands of the day are upon me with work emails, phone calls, and text messages. I find Jesus' message of hope during this time of day to be the loudest.

If you're not a morning person, no problem. You can find silence after all have gone to sleep, too! Give God your undivided attention even if it is for a short time today. Attempt to make this part of your everyday schedule, truly making it a priority and not a mundane task to check off your daily to-do list. Try to make it exciting by creating a cozy place for this time each day. It is sacred time set aside to spend with the One who cares for you deeply, knows your inner most thoughts and feelings, and knitted you together in your mother's womb (Psalm 139:13-14). When put this way, doesn't it make you want to give God the most precious time of your day? Prioritize time to find hope in His Word and to meditate on His promise.

The Garden of Growth

 Reflect on what you felt before, during, and after today's activity.

Day 70
Intentional Rest

So then, there remains a Sabbath rest for the people of God, for whoever has entered God's rest has also rested from his works as God did from his.
Hebrews 4:9-10

Previously, intentional rest was challenging for me. I would sit down and immediately felt I should be doing something productive and not wasting away on the couch watching my favorite TV show. I felt lazy. But I came to understand God intends for us to rest, rejuvenate, and recharge. Abraham Heschel, Jewish theologian and philosopher, said, "If you work with your mind, Sabbath with your hands. If you work with your hands, Sabbath with your mind." I heard this shared by my favorite Christian author and podcaster, Annie F. Downs. It made total sense to me when I heard it. I started looking for things I could do to Sabbath with my hands, since at my paying-the-bills job, I use my mind! I began working on puzzles, doing paint-by-numbers, planting flowers, and making homemade dog treats for Zoey and Gia. These are all things I enjoy doing with my hands, and they don't take much brain power. It gives my brain a rest but allows me to feel rejuvenated.

For today's activity, I encourage you to find an activity for your Sabbath. I've listed some activities for your hands and your mind below to get you started! I hope you find a way to incorporate observing Sabbath weekly, and that it allows you to feel rested, rejuvenated, and connected with God, yourself, and others.

<u>Hands</u>	<u>Mind</u>
<ul><li>Make flower arrangements</li><li>Write encouraging notes to friends or family</li><li>Cross stitch/knit/crochet</li><li>Garden</li></ul>	<ul><li>Research a topic you find interesting</li><li>Listen intently and reflect on the words of a song</li><li>Write a poem</li><li>Read a book</li></ul>

The Garden of Growth
• •

 Reflect on what you felt before, during, and after today's activity.

Day 71
Nourishing Comfort

Or do you not know that your body is a temple of the Holy Spirit within you, whom you have from God?
1 Corinthians 6:19

This activity is in honor of a woman named Pat, a cashier I met at Goodwill while writing this book! I was purchasing a few fragile items and Pat offered to wrap them for me, but I told her it wasn't necessary and she could put them in the milk crate I purchased. She packed the items tightly into the milk crate, bearing resemblance to a game of Tetris, keeping the items from moving around, and said, "Look there! I'm smart sometimes." I smiled at her and said, "I'm sure you're smarter more often than you give yourself credit for." As I paid, she leaned across the counter and said, "You know, I've been thinking about what you said. I probably don't give myself enough credit, but how can I when all I've known is what I've been told in relationships with men tearing me down my whole life and telling me how worthless I am? I used to love to cook, and I don't do it anymore because I'm scared I'll do it wrong."

Hearing her say this broke my heart, but I knew God was giving me an opportunity to pour love and encouragement into her life. I looked at her name tag and put my hands on top of her hands laying on the counter. I then leaned into the counter in the same way she did, and I said, "Pat, I'm sorry to hear about what you've faced. I know how it feels to be stripped of your confidence and not believe you're enough. But please don't let fear stop you from doing the things you love and what brings you joy! I bet you make a delicious meal with bites bursting with flavor. I hope you will go home tonight, make your favorite meal, and be reminded of how much you love doing it and be filled with the joy it once brought you!" As her eyes welled up with tears, she smiled and said, "I hope you have a good day, and you need to come back here more often."

In honor of Pat, it seems fitting to cook your favorite meal for today's activity. Prepare something you recall bringing you joy, comfort, nourishment, and satisfaction. It may even be nostalgic. If you prefer to bake, bake something instead of cooking and make your favorite dessert! And if you prefer not to cook or bake and the kitchen is not your favorite place in the house, do what my sweet momma does and make reservations.

The Garden of Growth

 Reflect on what you felt before, during, and after today's activity.

Day 72
Embrace Connection

I therefore, a prisoner for the Lord, urge you to walk in a manner worthy of the calling to which you have been called, with all humility and gentleness, with patience, bearing with one another in love, eager to maintain the unity of the Spirit in the bond of peace.
Ephesians 4:1-3

It is possible while engaged with your abuser, you experienced isolation from your friends or family. Maybe you weren't completely isolated, but you didn't have as close of a connection as you once did. If it happened to you, I'm sorry the enemy tried to take you down by keeping you from your loved ones. However, I hope you aren't holding onto any shame or guilt because of this, as unfortunately, it's not an unusual tactic used by abusers. Let's focus today's activity on embracing connection with others as God's Word encourages us to do!

Connecting and embracing others can be difficult, especially if you are engaging in new relationships after leaving your abuser. If this is out of your comfort zone, I encourage you to be bold and courageous today by reaching out to someone and making plans with them. You can make plans to have coffee or dinner together, or if you're more of the active type and the weather permits, invite someone to join you for a walk and have a conversation to get to know each other better. Finding and building adult friendships is difficult, but this is a way you can challenge yourself to be bold, confident, resilient, and try to start trusting others again! Who knows, this could lead to a beautiful, lifelong friendship because you were bold and confident and reached out and embraced the opportunity to build a connection.

The Garden of Growth

 Reflect on what you felt before, during, and after today's activity.

Day 73
Laughter as Medicine

*A joyful heart is good medicine,
but a crushed spirit dries up the bones.*
Proverbs 17:22

Raise your hand if you've ever laughed hard enough that your eyes or your bladder leaked. *Raises hand* Whoops! Laughter is so contagious, isn't it? It really is medicine for the soul. My favorite is when I get laughing extra hard to where no sound is even coming out and the tears are rolling down my cheeks and the pee is rolling down...okay, okay, I couldn't resist. Laughter fills me with such joy, gives me hope, and reminds me not to become bogged down with life, completely forgetting to enjoy it. Laughter is good for our hearts, as the Scripture says. I find it interesting how diverse people's humor is. My mom finds my brother's humor to be incredibly hilarious, and while I don't understand his humor, he sure can get her laughing, and I love to see her laugh and enjoy life. I'm not sure if others agree with me or not, but I think I'm funnier since the onset of my healing journey. I laugh at stuff I do and say often and have learned not to take myself so seriously.

Today, I thought it would be enjoyable for you to engage in an activity that hopefully brings you loads of laughter. Consider options such as watching your favorite comedy movie or sitcom, attending a stand-up comedy show, or streaming a comedy special from the comforts of home. A few comedians with clean humor I enjoyed watching in the past are Anita Renfroe, Chonda Pierce, and Leanne Morgan. You could also play Catch Phrase, Pictionary, or other improv games with family or friends. Finally, you could hang out with friends you find to be funny and whose company you enjoy. I have a funny friend, and regardless of what is going on in life, if I'm with her, I'm sure to bust a stitch with laughter! Whichever option you choose today, I hope you get a dose of the best laughter in town.

The Garden of Growth
• •

 Reflect on what you felt before, during, and after today's activity.

Day 74
Refute the Lies

See to it that no one takes you captive by philosophy and empty deceit, according to human tradition, according to the elemental spirits of the world, and not according to Christ.
Colossians 2:8

I hope these last few days of activities have been fun for you! As I brainstormed what to write in this section, I typed a page full of ideas and developed a mixture of thought-provoking, vulnerable, and challenging activities, but I threw in a few easy, life-giving, freeing, and silly activities, too! I hope you are finding joy in the mundane as you work through this section.

Abusers are known to tear down their victims by stripping them of self-confidence, filling them with self-doubt, and feeding them lies about what people say or think about their character. The longer the relationship continues, the further the victim is buried under lies about who they are. There are two parts to today's activity. First, in your journal make two columns. In the first column, make a list of the lies your abuser told you about who you are or what you did/didn't do when you would spend time together. In the second column, refute the lies with truth. For example, if your abuser fed you the lie of you being unlovable, that would go in column one. Then, in column two, you would write the truth: you are loveable because God loves you, your friends love you, and your co-workers enjoy working with you. I hope this activity will serve as a record of what you have been told. When those lies start to creep into your mind and you're having a dark moment, you can go straight to this list and see the truths laid out right in front of you! Declare it today: you will not be taken captive by the lies of the enemy!

Today's activity is deep and vulnerable. I know you can do it, but you might return to it later and work through it again or use it to dig even deeper. It has the potential to bring up difficult emotions, and it's okay to feel them. Let the emotions flow as you work through this exercise. Take breaks when you need to, listen to your body, and do what feels best for you in this stage of your personal healing.

The Garden of Growth

Reflect on what you felt before, during, and after today's activity.

Day 75
Joyful Dancing

Praise the Lord!
Praise God in his sanctuary;
praise him in his mighty heavens!
Praise him for his mighty deeds;
praise him according to his excellent greatness!
Praise him with trumpet sound;
praise him with lute and harp!
Praise him with tambourine and dance;
praise him with strings and pipe!
Praise him with sounding cymbals;
praise him with loud clashing cymbals!
Let everything that has breath praise the Lord!
Praise the Lord!
Psalm 150

The Lord loves to hear His children praise Him through song and dance. Psalm 150 is the first long Scripture I memorized at church camp when I was a teenager. I can close my eyes and hear it being read at the beginning of a song called, "Let Everything That Has Breath," originally sung by Matt Redman. I love music and love how worship music has evolved through the years. Although, I do still appreciate the old hymns, because they remind me of precious times with my grandparents when we sang together. Dancing, on the other hand, has never been a talent of mine! Let's be real, I have no rhythm. It's pretty comical. Now, I said it's comical, but I didn't say I don't do it! I crank up my speakers and dance when I clean the house. I do keep my windows closed to avoid embarrassing myself, but dancing while I clean house keeps me energized, focused, and in the mood to finish the task.

For today's activity, in the words of the music group Technotronic, it's time to "Pump Up the Jam" and dance! Let loose, feel free, spark energy, be silly, and create excitement! By my own research throughout my personal healing journey, I learned that when I intentionally move my body, it's considered a form of somatic therapy, which is a form of therapy connecting the mind and the body. I'm increasing endorphins, elevating my mood, reducing stress and anxiety, creating body awareness, allowing emotional release, and most importantly, encouraging self-expression. If you're not someone who dances regularly, perhaps this activity feels uncomfortable at first, but I encourage you to do it anyway. Grow through the uncomfortable, silly exercises because I'm sure you are loads of fun, my friend, and we all need a little fun in our lives. Go ahead, close the windows, crank up the music, and dance as if nobody's watching, because frankly, it's nobody's business!

The Garden of Growth
• •

 Reflect on what you felt before, during, and after today's activity.

Day 76
Building Courage

*Be strong, and let your heart take courage,
all you who wait for the Lord!*
Psalm 31:24

Everyone harbors fears, whether they're afraid of heights, public speaking, failure, spiders, snakes, or being alone or abandoned! Overcoming these fears demands trust in God, the willingness to do self-work, and tremendous courage. Recalling a previous day's devotion (Day 43–Conquering Fear), God does not give us a spirit of fear (2 Timothy 1:7), so fear is from the enemy. To overcome those fears, it demands facing them head on, not allowing them a seat at the table.

The task for today's activity is to work towards overcoming fear(s), building courage, and believing God is greater than the fear. Identify a current fear you have and jot it down in your journal. Next, write down two or three ways you can confront it by facing it head on. After you have a few possible solutions written down, commit to a date and time when you plan to carry out the actions to combat those fears. I recommend having someone join you for each undertaking to combat your fear. This will help actively encourage you and hold you accountable. If any or all of this sounds overwhelming, take time to talk it through with the Lord and let Him guide your mission plan. I believe in you! Joshua 1:9 tells us we are strong and courageous and to not be afraid because the Lord is with us. Take heart in Joshua's words.

The Garden of Growth

 Reflect on what you felt before, during, and after today's activity.

Day 77
Step-by-Step

He makes me lie down in green pastures.
He leads me beside still waters.
He restores my soul.
He leads me in paths of righteousness
for his name's sake.
Psalm 23:2-3

As you've read, growth and healing are both processes and not ones that follow a linear fashion. There is a path, but it is often a winding path. When I read through Psalm 23, it is highly calming to my soul. It presents me with an image of rest, peace, and tranquility. Imagine lying in the fluffiest, softest, and bug-free grass near a stream lightly and calmly flowing with the sun shining on your face. While imagining, take a deep breath. Wow! What a treat.

If you're not familiar with guided walking meditations, today's activity will require a little research before diving in. Guided walking meditations are a great way to connect with God's creation and appreciate all the beauty it has to offer. During a guided walking meditation, an instructor guides you through mindfulness while helping you focus your awareness and pay attention to the activity of walking itself. If you have an app such as Calm or Headspace, you can find guided walking meditations within the app. If you don't have access to either of those apps or something similar, open a browser on your phone and look up "guided walking meditations." It will pull up several websites with an audio player embedded or a link to video walking meditations for you to play. Many of these will be available at no charge. After you finish your guided walking meditation session, see if you can describe your own guided practice in a way reflective of the peace and tranquility Psalm 23 provides.

The Garden of Growth

 Reflect on what you felt before, during, and after today's activity.

Day 78
Celebrating You

*She opens her mouth with wisdom,
and the teaching of kindness is on her tongue.*
Proverbs 31:26

In the past, I wasn't the best at receiving compliments. I would discount someone's compliment by saying, "Stop" or "Oh, really?" I didn't do this to be rude or reject them; I did it because I was full of self-doubt and viewed myself through the lens of a negative self-image. If someone gave me a compliment, I instantly thought they were lying to me. Upon reflection, it makes me sad to think about how negatively I viewed myself—my body, my accomplishments, my work ethic, and my personality. I didn't have a positive self-image, so why and how could someone outside of me see anything good in me?

Today is about celebrating you. It's not about others celebrating you, but it's about you celebrating you. We teach kindness by first being kind to ourselves. God expects us to be kind to one another and being kind to one another includes being kind to ourselves. For today's activity, look at yourself in the mirror and give yourself at least three compliments. If you can do more, do it! These compliments should have depth to them.

The only one who knows you better than yourself is God, so dig deep and give yourself the compliments only you would know to give yourself. It can feel weird looking at yourself in the mirror and doing this. I get it. I felt weird when I did it at first, too. I did self-work in this area and now when someone compliments me, I follow up with, "Thank you," and I *actually* believe it. I hope you will come back to this activity and do it often, not just once and move on. Practicing this exercise regularly will start to rebuild your confidence and restructure your belief patterns about how you see yourself.

The Garden of Growth

 Reflect on what you felt before, during, and after today's activity.

Day 79
Who You Are

In him we have obtained an inheritance, having been predestined according to the purpose of him who works all things according to the counsel of his will, so that we who were the first to hope in Christ might be to the praise of his glory. In him you also, when you heard the word of truth, the gospel of your salvation, and believed in him, were sealed with the promised Holy Spirit, who is the guarantee of our inheritance until we acquire possession of it, to the praise of his glory.
Ephesians 1:11-14

Today's activity is fairly simple, but I suggest taking the time to reflect after you complete it. In your journal, rewrite Ephesians 1:3-14 replacing "us," "our," and "we" with "me," "my," and "I" (or your name). This Scripture is all about who God says you are, your identity in Christ, and the blessings He bestows upon His beloved children. I did this exercise, reflected on it for the days and weeks following, and it positively impacted me. Knowing God is for me and desires to bestow His love and blessings on me and my life is meaningful. What made me especially emotional from this passage is He predestined me for adoption to Himself. I'm chosen. *He chose me*. The King of Kings and Lord of Lords *chose me!* He wants *me* as His own and desires to have a personal relationship with *me*. What a display of the kindness and gentleness of the Lord. I hope you have a positive outcome with this activity and recognize you are chosen and never forsaken because God says you are His beloved.

The Garden of Growth

Reflect on what you felt before, during, and after today's activity.

Day 80
Celestial Serenity

Praise him, sun and moon,
praise him, all you shining stars!
Praise him, you highest heavens,
and you waters above the heavens!
Let them praise the name of the Lord!
For he commanded and they were created.
Psalm 148:3-5

The vastness of the universe has perpetually been miraculous to me. When I took astronomy in school, I never could point out the Big Dipper or any of the constellations, but I was amazed how everyone in the whole world was looking at the same sky. I'm still in awe at all God created and to know He still cares about me and I am still valuable to Him. I'm a tiny blip in this universe, but He intricately designed me and deeply loves me. Gazing up at a clear night sky when the moon is shining and the stars seem brighter than the sun, is a gift that is continuously giving.

For today's activity, go encounter this gift. If you live within driving distance of a location with a totally open, clear view of the sky, I highly recommend driving there. Feel free to take a close friend or family member along with you on this adventure if you feel nervous or uneasy about going somewhere secluded and dark, especially if it's an unfamiliar place. Allow yourself to be absorbed into the night sky and imagine God is holding you in His mighty hand and telling you the story of when He intimately knitted you together and the plans He has for your future. Let Him express love, encouragement, and comfort and show you how much you mean to Him. Allow Him to fill the deepest voids within you. I pray you feel His divine presence during today's activity.

The Garden of Growth

Reflect on what you felt before, during, and after today's activity.

Day 81
Quiet Pause

*It is in vain that you rise up early
and go late to rest,
eating the bread of anxious toil;
for he gives to his beloved sleep.*
Psalm 127:2

It's official. I'm claiming the title—Queen of Naps. From what my mom and grandma tell me, I've unequivocally excelled at naps throughout my life. As an adult, I still love to nap, especially on the weekends or on my lunch break. I'm not a bed napper, though; I'm a couch napper. Something about afternoon naps on my couch hits different than a nap in my bed. I am guilty of saying I will take a quick twenty-minute power nap and it turns into an hour (or more) instead. Typically, I feel well rested when I wake up and I'm glad to have kicked the midafternoon slump. When I have a good night's rest or a good afternoon nap, I'm grateful because I know this is a way God specifically displays His love for me.

Today, if you can squeeze in a short twenty-minute nap to refresh your mind, I highly recommend it. Rest is a necessity when healing because healing is exhausting. If you're not a napper and you can't fall asleep in the middle of the day, try taking a few minutes to relax, unwind, and let your brain and nervous system rest. You have permission to sit in silence and stillness and do absolutely nothing else. Give yourself the time for a quiet pause in your day because the Lord God Almighty loves you more than you could ever ask, think, or imagine!

The Garden of Growth

 Reflect on what you felt before, during, and after today's activity.

Day 82
Deep Cleansing

But all things should be done decently and in order.
1 Corinthians 14:40

I find it refreshing the way clean spaces positively shift my perspective, take away the feeling of being overwhelmed, and project a sense of calm. On the other hand, a cluttered space does the opposite. When I wish to feel a quick, tangible sense of accomplishment and have a sliver of peace, I engage in decluttering around my house. I'll choose a room, a cabinet, a dresser, a basket, anything manageable to me. Then, I will sort through the items and decide if I'll keep them, throw them away, or donate them. Once I get going, it's hard to stop because it helps me feel exceptionally lighter and freer to get rid of things I'm not using and can donate for someone else to use instead.

God desires His children to keep order with *all* things! This includes our homes, lives, minds, and our personal relationship with Him. Today, focus on choosing an area of your life to declutter and deep clean. You may decide to choose a room or space in your home, evaluate the thoughts consuming your mind, assess what is standing in the way of a deeper connection with Jesus and/or your quiet time with Him, or take note of the people in your life and examine the value added by being in each other's lives. Whatever you decide to declutter and organize, keep this activity handy to return to when you want to find a little peace and you desire to evaluate what you're allowing into your sacred spaces. Some things may be hard to let go of both physically and emotionally, but you can take the time you need to complete this activity and have the hard conversations with God and yourself to determine what the best decision is for you.

The Garden of Growth

 Reflect on what you felt before, during, and after today's activity.

Day 83
Thrifted Treasures

And when they had eaten their fill, he told his disciples, "Gather up the leftover fragments, that nothing may be lost."
John 6:12

Yes, I understand yesterday's activity was about decluttering and getting rid of things no longer serving a purpose and taking up space, but c'mon! Thrifting is my favorite. It's where someone's trash becomes someone else's treasure. Oh, it just clicked. Now I understand why I'm constantly having to declutter.

You've been doing significant introspection, self-work, and critical thinking. I thought it would be fun to incorporate something fun and a little quirky. This activity would be fun to do with a close friend or family member to spend quality time together. Put on an outfit you feel confident in, grab your keys, choose your favorite thrift store in town, and start driving! Once you get there, browse the store for an item you feel represents your growth and healing journey so far, whether it's a coffee mug with a cute saying (we can never have enough cute coffee mugs), a home décor piece you can style on a shelf, or a comfy, cute T-shirt you can relax in. Whatever item you choose, I hope when you see it in the months and years to come, it will ignite joy and happiness upon acknowledging your progress and growth!

Let's add a bonus to this activity: if you want to take it a step further, write a short elevator speech about your item, explaining why you chose it, what emotion it sparks in you, and how it relates to your healing. You never know when you will have the opportunity to share your story with someone and the inspiration it could spark within them to embark on their own path to healing.

The Garden of Growth

Reflect on what you felt before, during, and after today's activity.

Day 84
Lift Your Voice

About midnight Paul and Silas were praying and singing hymns to God, and the prisoners were listening to them...
Acts 16:25

To summarize Acts 16, Paul and Silas were accused of disturbing the city after they encountered a demon-possessed girl and Paul proceeded to cast the demon out of the girl. The men were beaten and imprisoned. Paul and Silas were full of despair and anguish for being imprisoned and not able to continue preaching the gospel, but despite their circumstances, they chose to sing praises to the Lord, which eventually led to their freedom.

For myself, I have found words are powerful, and music is healing. Music has been a significant part of my healing. Listening to worship music and shouting praise to the heavens, even if it's from within my house or my car, is powerful. According to James 2:19, Satan and his demons are fearful and tremble at the sound of Jesus' name. This is why singing praises to the Lord and saying the name of Jesus are powerful tools to ward off the enemy and his forces. For today's activity, blast the praise and worship music and sing along with it for as long as you want! You don't need to have an amazing singing voice—simply lift a joyful shout of praise unto the Lord, as Psalm

98:4 tells us to do! We can sing in times of despair and anguish or in times of joy and contentment. If it's uncomfortable, push forward and keep singing and you will become more courageous and brave each time. Plus, according to the book of Revelation, there is constant singing and praise going on in heaven and this activity helps prepare you for eternity with God!

The Garden of Growth

Reflect on what you felt before, during, and after today's activity.

Day 85
Heavenly Hugs

And God saw everything that he had made, and behold, it was very good. And there was evening and there was morning, the sixth day.
Genesis 1:31

Our heavenly Father created everything and saw it was very good! This includes the fur babies of the world! There have been countless studies done (through John Hopkins, University of Leeds, Cambridge University, and National Institutes of Health) revealing interaction with animals reduces stress. Animals are also good for providing unconditional love and comfort. I've mentioned my fur babies, Zoey and Gia, a few times throughout this book. Due to the proven benefits, I added this activity, which embraces snuggle time with your fur babies.

For today's activity, set aside some special time to bond and connect with your animal. Whether it is brushing your cat, playing fetch with your dog, or snuggling up on the couch with your cat and your dog, obsessively giving them petties and scratchies! I know when I'm sitting on the couch snuggling my pups and I look at them and they are completely at peace while sleeping, it brings me joy and fills my heart with contentment. Wait, there's more! I can hear some of you saying, "Awwww! I don't have an animal! What can I do instead to reap these same benefits?" I have a couple solutions! The first is for you to look into volunteering at a local animal shelter. Those animals need your love as much as you need theirs! Next, you could find a friendly neighbor with an animal you can love on. Another idea is to see if you have a cat café near you. This is a concept I've recently learned about—they have adoptable cats available, and you can go drink a chai and pet a cat. Oh! Now I have an idea: Kitten Chai Cat Café. I know! It's good, right? If all those solutions fail, and you can't do any of them because you are allergic to all animals, you can watch cute animal videos online. Some of those same studies have shown this is also beneficial. Seriously, who can resist a cute animal video? Let those feel-good endorphins multiply!

The Garden of Growth

 Reflect on what you felt before, during, and after today's activity.

Day 86
Calm Renewal

"The Lord will fight for you, and you have only to be silent."
Exodus 14:14

When I surrender control and let God fight my battles, it is a relaxing and reassuring place to rest. Knowing and understanding God takes on my enemies and my Goliaths, and I must only be silent and trust Him, reminds me how mighty and kind He is and how much He loves me. This takes the pressure off me needing to gear up and go into battle for myself. I know God surrounds me with protection. When I let God handle the hard stuff, I can relax and meditate calmly on His promises.

For the activity today, challenge your creative mind. Take your mind off any battles you thought required you to actively fight. Then, sit in a cozy spot—whether it's inside or outside doesn't matter. Most importantly, find a distraction-free environment, somewhere safe and comfortable. Once you have settled into the spot, in whatever position feels best, close your eyes. You can let your mind wander, but only allow it to wander to a relaxing destination. Use your imagination to create the most peaceful, relaxing, and comforting environment in your mind. This is an opportunity for you to dream and create your own utopia. There's remarkably more room in our minds to be creative when we surrender our struggles and battles to the One who can handle them all with ease and grace.

The Garden of Growth

 Reflect on what you felt before, during, and after today's activity.

Day 87
"No" is Not Mean

For the grace of God has appeared, bringing salvation for all people, training us to renounce ungodliness and worldly passions, and to live self-controlled, upright, and godly lives in the present age...
Titus 2:11-12

Guess what!? You're allowed to stand up for yourself and say no to ideologies and values not in alignment with yours. You're allowed to say no, and it doesn't make you a mean person. I was constantly concerned saying "no" to taking on an additional task at work or saying "no" to attending a get together with friends made me a mean person and people would be mad at me for the remaining days of my life. I lived in fear of losing my job if I told my boss I couldn't take on the additional task they were asking me to absorb. There is a kind way to say "no" while considering the feelings of others, but the point is, you don't have to be a yes-person. You can have boundaries, stand up for yourself, and take care of your needs before constantly taking on the needs of other people. Boundaries are set up to protect you and not intended to hurt the other person.

For today's activity, practice saying "no" in different ways. If possible, do this while looking in a mirror to also notice your facial expression. If you have a close friend or family member, ask them to role play a few different scenarios with you after you've practiced alone in the mirror. Have them ask you to take on an additional task or commit to attending an event, and the requirement is you must respond with "no". Take note, you don't need to provide a detailed explanation of why you are saying no to their request. You are an adult and as licensed counselor Jim Cress is known for saying, "Adults inform, children explain."[20] Lysa TerKeurst's book *Good Boundaries and Goodbyes*[21] is a book I gained valuable insight and inspiration from. I learned God wants us to have boundaries to protect us and limit who has access to the intimate parts of our life. Setting boundaries takes time and work and feels uncomfortable when you first start doing it. Let this be the start of a continuing work in progress to become comfortable with taking on only what you can handle and put boundaries in place to foster healthy and authentic connections with others.

The Garden of Growth
• •

 Reflect on what you felt before, during, and after today's activity.

Day 88
Smiling Faces

*Whoever pursues righteousness and kindness
will find life, righteousness, and honor.*
Proverbs 21:21

Complimenting people can turn someone's whole day around and give them a boost of confidence. There have been a handful of times I have made uncomfortable eye contact with a stranger. It's not my favorite thing to do because then what? Do I look away quickly, but if I do, will they think they have something on their face or toilet paper in their pants? But if I smile and hold eye contact, are they going to think I'm a weirdo or I'm flirting when, in reality, I'm uncomfortable? Honestly, I don't know how all those thoughts go through my mind in a short amount of time, but they do! I decided to work on training my brain to not put as much weight on what other people are thinking because I can't control their thoughts, anyway. I decided when I make eye contact with someone, I'll smile, and if they are close enough to me, I'll give them a compliment, such as they have a nice smile, they have beautiful eyes, or they are wearing a cute outfit. I can't identify an instance where I complimented someone, and they were offended by my kind words or genuineness. Generally, I think people appreciate it.

For today's activity, make it a point to give someone a compliment. This could be someone you work with, a person you encounter at the gym, or the cashier at the grocery store. It doesn't matter who you give the compliment to, just be sure to do it with authenticity and kindness. We speak many words in a day—too many, sometimes—so try to make it a point for some of those words to be life-giving and uplifting to a person in your path. Not only will this activity encourage someone, but it will encourage boldness, vulnerability and for you to pursue positive connection with others again.

The Garden of Growth

Reflect on what you felt before, during, and after today's activity.

Day 89
A Pathway to Healing

*Where there is no guidance, a people falls,
but in an abundance of counselors there is safety.*
Proverbs 11:14

Therapy has been part of my life since I was fifteen years old. I'm not ashamed to admit it as I believe there is significant value found in speaking to an unbiased party. These professionals are trained on the intricacies and inner workings of our brains. I find cognitive neuroscience to be fascinating and enjoy researching it when I can find the time. Personally, I find value in attending therapy sessions with someone trained outside of the church setting who still allows me to have my faith and belief system and share openly about it. My counselor provided me with useful tools and resources aiding greatly in my healing. I also had godly counsel through my community of Christian friends and fellow brothers and sisters in Christ. Based on the above Scripture, I understand there is safety with the avenues of therapy and my faith-filled mentors providing guidance.

Today's activity is about checking in with yourself to see if you are receiving the support you need for continued healing and moving towards healthy future relationships with others, romantic or otherwise, when this devotional journey ends. I hope you have found guidance, wisdom, and even a form of therapy through this devotional journey—don't let it end here. If you don't have someone lined up to talk with yet, try reaching out to a trusted friend, your doctor, or try Googling counselors or therapists in your area. If I can offer a piece of advice, it would be this: you don't have to stick with the first mental health professional you see. If you have the financial resources, try out a few and then make your decision. You want someone you feel comfortable sharing with, someone who allows you to speak freely, and someone who won't let you leave broken and bleeding until the next appointment.

If you can't afford counseling services, try to locate a Celebrate Recovery (CR) group meeting nearby, a support group, or contact a local domestic violence shelter to see what resources they have available. I pray God will lead you to the right place and to the right people for your healing to continue.

The Garden of Growth

 Reflect on what you felt before, during, and after today's activity.

Day 90
Words of Wisdom

*Listen to advice and accept instruction,
that you may gain wisdom in the future.*
Proverbs 19:20

You've made it to the last day of this ninety-day devotional journey! My goodness, I'm beaming with pride for you! I know working through this has taken a commitment of your time and energy, your courage and boldness, and your emotions and mental capacity. This was a brave adventure to embark on, not knowing exactly what you were diving into within these pages. Now, I present to you a final activity aiming to serve as a reflection on your journey from where you began to where you are now.

For today's activity, write a letter to the version of you from ninety days ago. Tell your former self what you've discovered, what's been revealed, how you feel, and the beauty you are beginning to uncover in your life on the other side of abuse and continued healing. If you want to take it one step further, share this letter with a trusted friend or family member for them to join in celebrating your healing, too!

There will forever be new things to learn about ourselves and ways to grow emotionally and spiritually with the Lord, as a result, the growth journey isn't over. We will keep growing. I hope you have gained hope and begun to feel healed and restored throughout these ninety days.

Before we part, allow me to share a message my friend sent when I was going through a dark season. I hope you find it helpful along your path the way I did. She said,

> *"Oh, sweet friend, know I am ALWAYS ALWAYS ALWAYS here. This world is way better with you in it than not. MY WORLD is better with you in it. I know you're facing tough stuff right now, but I'm with you. You're not alone no matter how much I know that brain of yours probably makes you think you are."*

I saved her text message in the Notes app on my phone to refer to when I need a loving reminder from a precious friend.

You're never alone. Please don't ever give up when a situation feels too heavy or insurmountable. Reach out to friends or family you trust and know are safe. Most importantly, turn your eyes upon Jesus and lean on the promises He provides. You are His masterpiece, and you are on this earth to fulfill God's plan and purpose for your life. If you're still breathing, He's not done. Allow Him to work in your life and give Him the glory and honor for all He has brought you through. My sweet friend, it's officially time to trust and believe you are fully known and deeply loved by God, and as your sister in Christ, I love you, too. Do you like hugs? I like hugs! I'm sending you a hug!

The Garden of Growth

Reflect on what you felt before, during, and after today's activity.

Notes

1. Peter Lord, Hearing God: Developing a Conversational Relationship with God (Nashville: Thomas Nelson, 1996), 44-45.

2. "Beware The Dangers of a Victim Mentality," The Gospel Coalition, last modified December 8, 2020, https://au.thegospelcoalition.org/article/beware-the-dangers-of-a-victim-mentality/.

3. Lysa TerKeurst, Joel Muddamalle, and Jim Cress "S1 E2 | Good Guilt vs. Destructive Shame," August 29, 2022, in Therapy and Theology, podcast, MP3 audio, 45:29, https://therapyandtheology.transistor.fm/episodes/good-guilt-vs-destructive-shame.

4. "Projection," Psychology Today, accessed November 6, 2023, https://www.psychologytoday.com/us/basics/projection

5. Gary Chapman, The Five Love Languages: How to Express Heartfelt Commitment to Your Mate (Chicago: Northfield Publishing, 1992).

6. "Triangulation: The Narcissists Best Play," PsychCentral, accessed February 9, 2024, https://psychcentral.com/blog/psychology-self/2019/10/triangulation-and-narcissism#1

7. "Triangulation from a Christian perspective," Jesus Alone, accessed February 9, 2024, https://thelordalone.com/2020/10/22/triangulation-from-a-christian-perspective/

8. "Narcissistic Baiting Examples And How To Respond," SimplyPsychology, accessed January 12, 2024, https://psychcentral.com/blog/psychology-self/2019/10/triangulation-and-narcissism#1

9. "Origin Of The Term Gaslighting," SimplyPsychology, last modified January 20, 2024, https://www.simplypsychology.org/origin-of-the-term-gaslighting.html

10. John McArthur, The McArthur Study Bible, 2nd Edition, English Standard Version, ESV (Nashville: Thomas Nelson, 2021), 823.

11. Rev. Keepers, Dustyn, Elizabeth, "The Samaritan Woman at the Well," Faithward, accessed on June 16, 2024, https://www.faithward.org/the-samaritan-woman-disciple-and-evangelist/?gad_source=1&gclid=CjwKCAjwmrqzBhAoEiwAXVpg000YWjP8wtzieSbgn2OzggeDNqC5ce28EMPL04mv4X0JUQKDwBm-SBoCgWoQAvD_BwE#_ftnref1.

12. "A Christian Approach to Complex PTSD," Seattle Christian Counseling, last modified November 14, 2019 https://seattlechristiancounseling.com/articles/a-christian-approach-to-complex-ptsd.

13. "Dissociative Disorders," Smoky Rain Counseling Services: Connecting to Heal, accessed March 8, 2024 https://www.smokyraincounseling.com/articles/dissociative-disorders/.

14. "Supporting Someone Who Keeps Returning to An Abusive Relationship," National Domestic Violence Hotline, accessed January 25, 2024, https://www.thehotline.org/resources/supporting-someone-who-keeps-returning-to-an-abusive-relationship/#:~:text=Leaving%20an%20abusive%20relationship%20is,who%20has%20never%20experienced%20abuse

15. "What the Bible says about Cognitive Dissonance (From Forerunner Commentary)," Bible Tools, accessed March 8, 2024 https://www.bibletools.org/index.cfm/fuseaction/Topical.show/RTD/cgg/ID/1926/Cognitive-Dissonance.htm

16. "What the Bible says about Cognitive Dissonance (From Forerunner Commentary)," Bible Tools, accessed March 8, 2024 https://www.bibletools.org/index.cfm/fuseaction/Topical.show/RTD/cgg/ID/1926/Cognitive-Dissonance.htm

17. "I Doubt They Genuinely Repented," Bible Love Notes, accessed March 8, 2024 https://biblelovenotes.blogspot.com/2016/03/i-doubt-they-genuinely-repented.html.

18. Julie Roys and Diane Langberg "Episode 102 | Diane Langberg: Where is God When There's Abuse?," June 28, 2022, in The Roys Report, podcast, MP3 audio, 12:56, https://julieroys.com/podcast/diane-langberg-where-is-god-when-theres-abuse/.

19. "About Us," Celebrate Recovery, accessed April 23, 2024, https://celebraterecovery.com/about/.

20. Lysa TerKeurst, Joel Muddamalle, and Jim Cress "S1 E10 | Dealing With Anxiety," August 29, 2022, in Therapy and Theology, podcast, MP3 audio, 14:55, https://therapyandtheology.transistor.fm/episodes/dealing-with-anxiety.

21. Lysa TerKeurst, Good Boundaries and Goodbyes: Loving Others Without Losing the Best of Who You Are (Nashville: Thomas Nelson, 2022).

About the Author

Heather is a writer, speaker, dog-lover, domestic violence advocate, and most importantly, a child of God. She is passionate about empowering women to set healthy boundaries and know their self-worth. She strives to build a community of people around her that are authentic and life-giving. Heather is a homebody who enjoys hosting, frothy coffee, warm blankets, puppy snuggles, being cozy, and sitting on the patio listening to nature.

Heather is a creative entrepreneur at heart. She finds great joy in uplifting and encouraging others to pursue their personal and professional goals. She wholeheartedly believes, "If we can dream it, God can do it."

She places a strong emphasis on mental health and values honesty, transparency, and vulnerability. Heather has a heart for young women and, when given the opportunity, she strives to make them feel seen and heard.

Heather loves events where she can engage with like-minded women who are willing to discuss hard topics such as: the many types and facets of abuse, trauma, healing, and mental health.

If you're interested in booking her for your next live event, send an email to heathernjustice1@gmail.com or get in touch via the *Contact* form on Heather's website at www.heathernjustice.com.

www.ingramcontent.com/pod-product-compliance
Lightning Source LLC
Chambersburg PA
CBHW020458030426
42337CB00011B/145